WWII

THE INVASION
OF POLAND

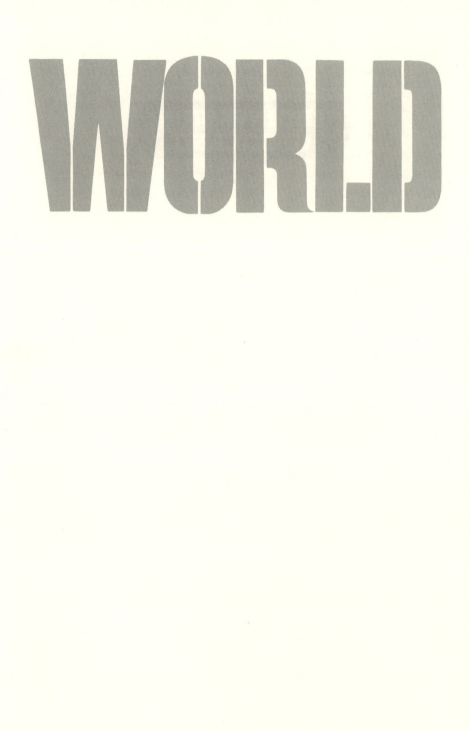

**TURNING POINTS OF**

# THE INVASION OF POLAND

## ALAN SAUNDERS

A GROLIER COMPANY

FRANKLIN WATTS ▪ 1984
NEW YORK ▪ LONDON ▪ TORONTO ▪ SYDNEY

FOR MY JASON, WHOSE EXCITEMENT
IN HISTORY IS JUST UNFOLDING

Photographs courtesy of:
Culver Pictures, Inc.: pp. 9, 16, 27, 42; National Archives: p. 48;
AP/Wide World: pp. 61, 64, 84, 94; UPI: pp. 73, 77; U.S. Army: p. 87.

Maps courtesy of Vantage Art, Inc.

Library of Congress Cataloging in Publication Data

Saunders, Alan.
The invasion of Poland.

(Turning points of World War II)
Bibliography: p.
Includes index.
Summary: Traces the history of Poland, emphasizing
events leading to the September, 1939, invasion of
Poland by the armies of Germany and Russia.
1. Poland—History—1918-1945—Juvenile literature.
2. Poland—Relations—Germany—Juvenile literature.
3. Germany—Relations—Poland—Juvenile literature.
[1. Poland—History—1918-1945. 2. World War, 1939-1945
—Campaigns—Poland] I. Title. II. Series.
DK4401.S28 1984          943.8'04          84-10367
ISBN 0-531-04864-0

# CONTENTS

# POLAND:
# THE ANCIENT
# NATION

**O**f many a place it has been said that it was more a state of mind than a specific location. Among nations Poland is perhaps the best example of this view. It is only if we accept this, that we can begin to understand the idea that is Poland, and what—through more than a thousand years—this idea, this nation, has come to mean to its people. Given that knowledge, the terrible days of September 1939 transcend the simple thought of two huge armies relentlessly swallowing a technologically backward, smaller foe. With that background we can also begin to understand the reason for the ferocity displayed both by the invaders, Germany and Russia, and by their hapless victim, Poland.

For the Germans, Poland's existence had always been a thorn, an ostensibly weak neighbor who nevertheless managed time after time to successfully challenge imperial Germany's policy of "Drang nach Osten," its expansionist drive to the east. For the Russians the memory of repeated Polish domination of large segments of their territory, once including Moscow itself, was an insult to their sense of national sovereignty that needed to be washed in Polish blood.

The first pages of Polish history record a shaky beginning in the tenth century. Beginning in 900 A.D., the Polians, a tribe of field dwellers ruled by the Piast family, managed to unify the surrounding tribes under their control, a process that took several generations.

In 963, as a result of an attack on their land by a German princeling, the Polians came in full contact with the Christian world of Western Europe. The attack had not been sanctioned by then German Emperor Otto I, and Mieszko Piast, the reigning head of the Polians, wisely took full advantage of this fact. After two encounters where his men were defeated, Mieszko, realizing that Poland's security would be found only under the umbrella of the German empire, took himself to Otto and declared his lands a vassal state to the emperor. In return Otto conferred upon Mieszko the title of Duke of Poland, thus effectively curbing further forays from the German princes.

Poland at the time, however, was a pagan country. Fearing that under the pretext of Christianization his lands might again be invaded by the Germans, Mieszko quickly chose to become a Catholic. The quickest way to do this was to marry a Catholic princess. He did not have far to go. In neighboring Bohemia—now part of Czechoslovakia—he found Dubravska, a Catholic princess, whom he promptly married in 965. Within a year, by dint of much persuasion, some of it rather forceful, he turned Poland into a Catholic country. With exceptional vision Mieszko had quickly grasped that the real powers of medieval Europe were the Church and the German emperor. He had made peace with the emperor, but to be safe, he made his lands over to the Pope, thereby putting Poland dircetly under the Pope's protection, even though he had earlier declared Poland a vassal state of the emperor. Thus, with these masterful strokes, he became an ally of the Germanic federation and he assured Poland of Rome's support.

Having defined his western borders in his agreement with Otto, Mieszko turned northward and southward, concluding agreements with the Scandinavian kingdoms and with Hungary. Securing his eastern border, however, proved to be a problem.

Fighting had regularly occurred between pagan Pole

and pagan Russian. The arrival of Christianity was to make matters worse. In the sixth century, the Catholic Church had been divided into two branches for political considerations. One branch was centered in Rome and was known as the Roman Catholic Church. The other branch took root in the east, in Byzantium, and became known as the Byzantine, or Eastern, rite. When the Russians became Christian, they took on the ritual of the Eastern, Byzantine Church, rather than that of Rome, so religion seemed only to accentuate the differences between Russian and Pole, between the east and the west. Although Russians and Poles were both Slavic people, they polarized even their religious beliefs into antagonisms that prevail to this day.

Thus, from its very inception, Poland has stood between the Russian hammer and the German anvil. That this position forged a warlike nation of indomitable spirit, there can be no doubt. The very topography of the land has forced the Poles to become either warriors or serfs. Most countries have natural boundaries, boundaries made of mountains, rivers, or seas. Obstacles such as these confine people to a given area, allowing them to develop the distinct characteristics from which nationhood is formed. Then, as now, Poland had forests, plains, and marshes as its eastern and western borders. Poland's rivers, rather than being obstacles, have been waterways giving access to the land. For the industrious Germans it was not hard to envision fertile Poland in much the same way as Americans in the nineteenth century might have conceived of their western territories. For the Russians, too, Poland loomed as an agricultural land whose rich, easily traversed plains made it the natural passageway to the wealth of the Western world.

For Poland peace with the German empire did not survive Otto I. Otto II attempted an invasion but was repulsed. Poland—not yet a unified nation—had twice locked horns with Germany in less than one generation. And Russia in the east had successfully attacked, taking several Polish strongholds on the San and Bug rivers.

Mieszko's son, Boleslav I, however, was soon to remedy both situations. Otto III recognized that an independent Poland under its own king would be better as an ally than a vassal state, since he would not have to subsidize it. And Otto III was proved right. Under Boleslav not only did Poland officially become a country but also, in a burst of expansion, it reached a territorial extent that closely parallels its present borders. Most of the conquered lands were pagan, and with the Polish soldiers also came the cross, a pleasing fact to both emperor and Pope.

For the next three centuries the Polish kings encouraged Germanic immigration to their largely underpopulated lands, a policy that brought both great benefits and grave consequences. The new settlers were more skilled and educated than the Poles, and they used their abilities well in founding new towns and villages. Although German, they often had no great love for their former overlords and happily accepted Polish rule. Later their presence would give rise to German territorial claims over the lands they inhabited, and as the differences between Pole and German became more acute, a mutal antipathy would develop.

The country Mieszko I and Boleslav I had put together was greatly weakened by a policy begun by Ladislav Herman, a later Polish king. This policy was the institution of appanage, which basically consisted of the king dividing the country among all his sons rather than leaving the throne and its power to just one. In theory all brothers were subjects of the eldest, but in practice this was not really so. The result was that instead of a single nation, Poland became a series of semi-independent duchies, ruled by a weak king, hardly a match for a growing and expanding Germany. Slowly the country began to disintegrate. Pomerania was lost, and parts of Silesia also went to the Germans.

Losing territory in the west, the Poles sought conquests in the east, rashly attacking then pagan Prussia. Too weak to conquer Prussia alone, however, they called in the German order of the Teutonic Knights. Originally founded as a religious-military order during the Crusades, the Knights had outlived their original charitable purpose and had become a private army of formidable strength, the vanguard of Christian advance into the heathen lands of northeastern Europe. Prussia at the time being pagan territory—except for a few Christian enclaves—fell well within the defined purpose of the Knights. After a number of encounters, the Knights secured several strongholds. Much to the surprise and consternation of the Poles, after fortifying their positions, they refused to turn over the newly conquered lands to the Polish king. Instead, in 1226, their Grand Master declared Prussia a part of the German empire, thus incurring for the Order the eternal enmity of Poland. For fifty years the Knights labored to destroy the native Prussians. Backed by large contingents of German immigrants, they finally supplanted the pagan Prussians with Christian Germans, who not only took over the land but also soon began to call themselves Prussians, thus renouncing their former loyalty and thwarting the hopes of the Polish king as well.

But Poland's troubles were not over. Soon a much more terrible enemy was to appear. From the plains of Tataria in Russia, the Golden Horde—an immense force of savage Mongol horsemen headed by Batu Khan, a grandson of Genghis Khan—surged westward, crushing all resistance in its path. Poland, too, was engulfed by the Mongols, but it was in Poland that the Golden Horde found its victories too costly, and its tidal wave was forced to recede. Yet for the next two hundred years fear of the Tatar specter would strongly influence Polish policy and thought.

Reeling from these blows, never quite able to recover from one before the next one fell, the Polish state continued to crumble. Too weak to attempt conquest alone, the Poles in 1308 once again asked for the Teutonic Knights' help, this time to recover Pomerania, the country's only province with access to the sea. As before, the Knights' assistance proved too costly. After defeating Poland's enemies, they massacred the Polish garrison at Danzig, Pomerania's principal city, and seized the province for themselves. Here, as in Prussia earlier, they followed a policy of Germanization by immigration.

For close to four hundred years, the dynasty of the Piasts had been ruling Poland, while the nation became progressively weaker. At the end of the fourteenth century, a new dynasty would assume power and bring Poland to its greatest splendor. Before this, however, the last Piast would redeem his ancient name and return to Poland some of its former glory. Casimir the Great, by skillful diplomacy, settled his country's western borders with a solution that lasted for over four hundred years. In the east, by force of arms, he secured the cooperation of a number of pagan Lithuanian princes, thus paving the way for the Lithuanian dynasty that was to follow. Internally he set up a system of government, which by its flexibility, enabled the diverse people now coming under Polish rule to live peacefully together.

The towns, many of which had large German populations, were granted special tribunals, and other commercial interests received special safeguards. The nobles until Casimir had had a series of patchwork agreements with the crown. The king now formally recognized the agreements as prerogatives for all the nobility. With these moves he strengthened both the nobility and the merchant class, but he also bound them more closely to the crown.

Casimir's lenient policy toward the Jews, who were generally persecuted in Europe at the time, led to substantial Jewish migrations to Poland. The Jews not only increased a sparse population but also brought with them needed skills and knowledge. By all these measures Casimir was able to leave to his successors a still lame, yet quickly healing Poland—a legacy of which the Jagiellonian kings who were soon to rule Poland would take full advantage.

Casimir, however, failed in one undertaking. Even though he had been married three times, no son had been produced. Therefore, having no male heir of his own, he destined the crown for his nephew Louis of Hungary. Louis

Casimir the Great strengthened Poland
in the late fourteenth century by settling
his country's borders and establishing
an effective system of government.

would prove a poor ruler whose main ambition was to ensure that his daughters (for he had no sons either) would wear a royal crown. To obtain the consent of the Polish nobility for his daughter to be crowned, he agreed to hold them free of taxation and to have all territorial offices become their exclusive property rather than the crown's. After much squabbling, his eleven-year-old daughter Jadwiga was accepted by the nobles as "King" of Poland. Then, as her consort, the nobility elected Jagiello, the pagan Grand Prince of Lithuania, who had agreed to place his lands under the Polish crown. A year later, in 1386, the couple was married, innagurating two centuries of Jagiellonian rule.

The decision to incorporate Lithuania into Poland in this manner was a wise one for both nations. Lithuania, a fragmented land ruled by many petty princes, had already been largely united by Jagiello. As a pagan land, its most dangerous enemy was the Teutonic Knights, Poland's old nemesis. The order—under the pretext of Christianization—was constantly enlarging its fiefdom at Lithuania's expense. Jagiello, though, agreed to become a Catholic and to Christianize his country himself, thus removing the ostensible reason for the Order's existence in Lithuania.

The Lithuanian nobles were granted the same privileges as their Polish brethren. The Eastern Christian Orthodox princes of Ruthenia were allowed to keep both their autonomy and their religious rites. They were asked only to swear their loyalty to the Polish crown.

Jadwiga, who had married at the age of twelve, ruled with her husband for thirteen years before she died giving birth to their only child. In those brief years, however, Jadwiga managed to become a great force for peace in a time of vast unrest. A measure of her efforts and successes can be gleaned from the fact that a movement to canonize her as a saint was started upon her death, a process that nearly six hundred years later is still important to many Poles. Jagiello, whose long reign lasted nearly fifty years, married three more times, producing a son and heir with his last wife.

Not long after Jagiello became king, the Order of the Teutonic Knights, which for a while had remained quiescent, began to stir again. Its advances eventually culminated in their encounter with Jagiello's troops at Tannenberg. There, in 1410, the Teutonic Knights suffered a decisive defeat at the hands of the Poles, a feat of arms that fanned great hopes in Polish hearts, and went far in strengthening the new Lithuanian ties.

Another epic day came at Harodlo, an ancient town on the river Bug. There, forty-seven Polish boyars, or nobles, each adopted a Lithuanian noble house, making of its men their brothers, vesting them with their own coats of arms, thus sharing privilege and rank. The result was an intermingling and fusing of Lithuanian-Polish nobility, a process whose results can be seen to this day.

At Harodlo, too, Jagiello proclaimed a first for Eastern Europe: no one could be imprisoned without trial. He also established another novel concept, that of an elective, rather than an inherited, monarchy. Although on the surface an elective monarchy seemed an excellent idea, much later it would, under the aegis of weak and venal men, create incredible dissension and open the way for Poland's disintegration.

For the next six generations, however, all Polish kings would be descendants of Jagiello. Like their sire, most were prudent, just, and brave. Under them Poland's sway would stretch from the Baltic to the Black Sea, from Germany deep into Russia, making it for a time the largest single state of Western Europe, a position the Poles would never forget.

It was in this period that Polish culture, trade, and learning flourished: universities were opened; Italian architects and artists were invited to the court; and scholars were encouraged by grants and teaching posts. Cracow acquired its fame as a center for the cloth trade, and Polish merchants traveled far and wide, returning to their land with new products. In a world beset with religious bigotry, the Jagiellonian kings offered refuge to all manner of dissenters. Under their protection Jews continued to flock to Poland from all parts of Europe, their contribution substantially helping the country to thrive. Protestants of every coloration found a haven there, too. The union with Lithuania was further cemented, and religious freedom plus a great deal of autonomy, made it possible for the diverse people in the realm to live peacefully together.

Yet the clouds of war would soon rise. At Tannenberg the Teutonic Order had been subdued, but it would soon rise again. The Knights marched against Poland, to be once more defeated. Their Prussian and Pomeranian fiefdoms rose against them with the support of the Polish army. Danzig greeted the entry of Polish troops with joy.

At the same time, two new threats appeared from the fearsome east: the Turkish Ottoman empire and a surging Moscow. In the south, in 1673, Vienna was besieged by the Turks, and a Polish army led by Jan Sobieski in a costly chivalrous gesture attacked and threw back the Ottoman horde.

To head off the threat of the Russians and Turks, the Poles organized the fugitive serfs who inhabited the Ukraine into military units. These fierce cossacks served Poland well. Only later did unkept promises and blind disregard for their rights turn the cossacks against Warsaw. For now, though, Poland was in its golden age.

The last Jagiello died childless in 1572. From this point on, the Polish crown was truly elective; Poland was now a royal republic. The king was elected by the Sejm, the Polish senate, and his choice of wife was dictated. The king's finances and the army—though ostensibly under his command—were in reality controlled by the nobility of the realm. Most importantly he was voiceless in the matter of his successor. The first elected king, a Frenchman, lasted only one year. When the throne of France became available by the death of his brother, he returned home. To say the least, this was not a good beginning for the idea of elective monarchy.

With the next king, a Hungarian, the Poles would fare better, if only for a short while. Stephen Bathory did much for Poland and justly ranks as one of its best kings. His reign was brief, scarcely eleven years, but he managed for a brief time to stem the Russian tide, which would soon envelop Poland. Through his efforts the vital issue of a seaport for Poland, at Danzig, was settled; the Jews were given their own parliament; and the restive cossacks were pacified. In the north, Bathory defeated the Russian horde under Ivan the Terrible, and with great vision he attempted to create a league to fight against the Turks. For a time it seemed as though the Jagiellonian star would also guide him. But in 1586, he suddenly died, and upon his death the flaws of the elective process became even more glaringly apparent.

The next king, Sigismund III, was a Swede who tried to unite in himself his father's Swedish crown and the one to which he had just been elected. But the Swedes objected and made war on Poland. Sigismund, in fact, proved to be quite a hindrance to both kingdoms, and Poland, being the most directly affected, suffered most. Indeed, Sigismund set the stage for Poland's decline over the next one hundred years or so. He and his successors were plagued with nearly every misfortune known to a nation, from foreign invasion to internal revolts. His attempts to Catholicize by force those elements that had strayed or were Orthodox met with failure. His attempts to gain the Swedish crown ended with Poland being invaded first by his kinsmen, then by the Russians for good measure. Although there was still a king on the Polish throne, the kingdom was now in reality an empty shell.

Not the least of the causes of this sad state was the "Liberum Veto," the right of any single member of the Sejm to utter the words "nie pozwalam," "I disapprove," and with this kill any act that might have been approved by the rest of the senate. With this weapon in hand, Poland's enemies, by bribery or coercion could and did, bring the country to a standstill. Bit by bit the lands that had been Poland's were par-

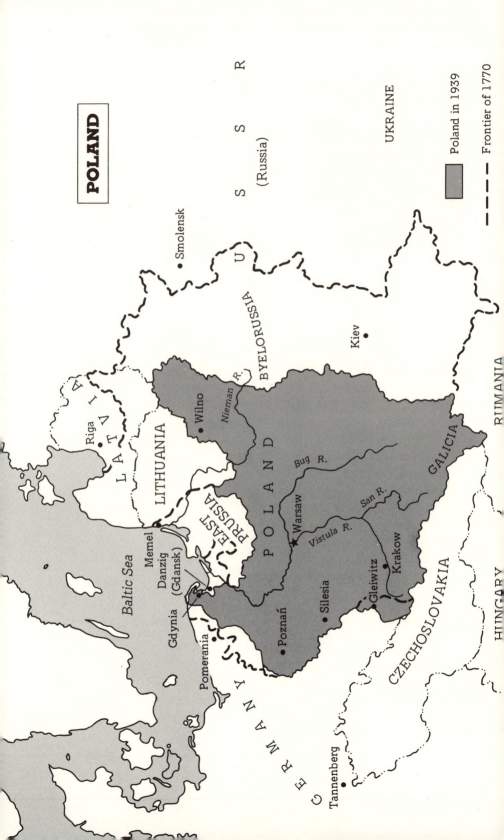

POLAND

Poland in 1939

Frontier of 1770

Smolensk

S   S   R

(Russia)

UKRAINE

U

BYELORUSSIA

Kiev

Riga

L   A   T   V   I   A

LITHUANIA

Wilno

Nieman R.

P   O   L   A   N   D

Bug R.

Warsaw

Vistula R.

San R.

GALICIA

Baltic Sea

Memel

Danzig
(Gdansk)

EAST
PRUSSIA

Gdynia

Pomerania

Poznań

Silesia

Gleiwitz

Krakow

CZECHOSLOVAKIA

HUNGARY

RUMANIA

G   E   R   M   A   N   Y

Tannenberg

celed out to her now conquering neighbors, and in 1772 the inevitable finally occurred.

In that year Prussia, Austria, and Russia legalized what they had in fact been doing, and officially apportioned one third of Poland to themselves. This shocked the nobility enough so that for the first time in generations they began to think of Poland as their country, not simply as the source of their own riches. As a result, governmental reform took place, and on May 3, 1791, a new constitution was approved and the Liberum Veto abolished.

But it was too late. Scarcely two years would pass before Prussia and Russia helped themselves to another third of Poland, leaving the remainder as little more than a vassal state. This time actual insurrection broke out, led by General Tadeusz Kosciuszko, a hero of the American Revolution.

Arriving in America a well-trained soldier, Kosciuszko immediately caught the eye of George Washington, who made him his adjutant. Later, as an American colonel, he had performed brilliantly in battles both at New York and at Yorktown. At the end of the war, a grateful Congress had made him both a general and an American citizen.

Returning to Europe, Kosciuszko served in the Polish army until the partitions forced him to assume a political role as well. As a leader he had unfortunately roused the suspicion of all neighboring monarchs by his American experience and his republican leanings, of which he made no secret while he was in Paris, asking for French help for Poland. Since his stay there coincided with one of the worst periods of the French Revolution, he returned home doubly tainted by that brush. As a result, the external help that Poland needed to defeat the combined Prussian-Russian efforts was withheld.

Left to their own devices, the Poles first gained some victories, but the force of greater arms and Polish dissension soon eliminated what advantage they had. On September 6, 1794, massed Russian troops overwhelmed the Warsaw garrison and massacred all Poles on their way to the city. Shortly

*Tadeusz Kosciuszko is known in America
as a hero of the Revolutionary War and
in Poland as the military leader who
opposed the Russian forces in 1794.*

after this debacle, at another battle, Kosciuszko himself was wounded and taken prisonor by the Russians. The Third Partition now took place, and with it Poland ceased to exist.

But although Poland, the country, was no more, the Polish spirit lived on. It lived chiefly in the officers and men of Kosciuszko's army, men who formed the Polish Legions and served Napoleon. They first campaigned in Italy, where one of their marching songs became the Polish national anthem. After that they served bravely in all the other fronts where the Little Corporal ranged. The hope of the Legions was that Napoleon would restore Poland. The emperor went so far as to create the Duchy of Warsaw, but then came the disaster of the Russian campaign of 1812, which destroyed the French army. With this defeat ended the possibility of a free Poland.

For the next hundred years Poland would continue to be subjugated, its people in the German sector being Germanized, those under Russian control Russified.

As the years went by and sporadic rebellions were squashed, the controls imposed by the foreign powers became tighter and tighter. Then in 1914 came World War I, and at the end of it, the long prayed-for miracle. Once more there was a place on the map called Poland.

# CHAPTER II

## POLAND REBORN: 1918-1938

**T**he end of World War I brought incredible gifts for Poland. First of all came the defeat and disintegration of the three powers that had partitioned it—Germany, Austria-Hungary, and Russia. Then world opinion proclaimed itself strongly in favor of a reborn Poland. President Woodrow Wilson's Fourteen Points, his vision of postwar Europe, expressly declared "the necessity of creating an independent Polish State." Not only that, thanks largely to the Polish Legions who had seen service in World War I, under Generals Jozef Pilsudski and Jozef Haller, Poland found herself not just free, but with the military might that would enable her to maintain that freedom.

With the gifts, though, also came the seeds of future destruction. The new Poland included territories that, while historically Polish, encompassed large populations of Russian and German origin. Poland, an intensely nationalistic nation, was bent on restoring historical Poland, the country that had existed in 1772—nearly one hundred fifty years earlier. That the population of those lands had substantially changed in that time, and that even greater changes were afoot were blithely ignored by the Poles—a cavalier neglect that would cost them very dearly just over twenty years later.

What Poland saw at the time was an opportunity to return to its former glory and even—if she played her cards right—

to a seat at the council of the great powers. And why not? Its soldiers had distinguished themselves in battlefields across Europe. Had not the Polish Legions constituted one of the bravest elements of Napoleon's Grand Army? Had not those Polish soldiers fought in subsequent wars so well that they earned the respect and admiration of all of Europe? Two of Poland's sons, Frederic Chopin and Ignazy Paderewski, musicians both, had changed the world with their work and done much to maintain the image of a conquered but proud nation, which while faced with incredible odds, nonetheless had proclaimed itself alive and filled with hope. Still, odds had been and still were overwhelming.

Ethnic Poland, that is, the people whose language, customs, and lands had always been Polish, unquestionably stood united. But what of the *other* Poles: the Ukranians, the White Russians, the Lithuanians, the Galicians, the Germans, the Jews? These—unlike the Italian-, French-, and German-speaking peoples who comprise the Swiss state—not only felt their separateness but had been actively discriminated against. In this the Poles were not alone, for they followed the practice of most other Eastern European nations, with the notable exception of Austria-Hungary. There, too, minority persecution was common, but not nearly as savagely practiced as in the neighboring lands.

Geographically, Poland stood as a tasty morsel between the jaws of Germany and Russia. An agricultural nation with no natural barriers or frontiers, Poland could not, like Switzerland, look to mountains, money, or a strong industry for protection. True, the Poles were fierce soldiers, but modern warfare—even in 1918—demanded more than raw courage, noble horses, and sharp swords. And Poland's industry, never mind her war industry, was negligible. What war itself had not destroyed, the Russians in their retreat had stripped. Whole factories had been loaded onto trains, and the trains driven eastward. Sometimes even the very rails had been ripped up behind them and carted off to Russia.

For these and other acts the Poles swore revenge, sadly

forgetting the immenseness of Russia and the huge armies it could command. Like a terrier Poland harried the Russian bear, which, stunned and bleeding from the wounds of the Bolshevik revolution and defeat in the war, howled in momentary impotence and anger. So Poland asked for and got from the victorious allies much of her old Russian lands. To these she would add the spoils of her victory in the 1920 Russo-Polish War. And, most unwisely, in an effort to Polonize them, it would bring Poles to these lands, giving them the good jobs and favored places. Not unnaturally this incurred the enmity and anger of the White Russians and Ukranians who inhabited these regions.

These people had originally viewed the arrival of the Poles, if not with wild enthusiasm, at least with a measure of tolerance and hope, for the Ukranians and the White Russians, too, were still smarting from over a century of harsh czarist rule. The Poles, however, dashed those hopes with their high-handed ways and as a result found themselves overlords of a surly and resentful people.

To the west Poland did not fare much better. Much of the German land they recovered was and had been German. That these territories had been taken from Poland a century and a half earlier was not of great import to their present German inhabitants, many of whom could point to local tombstones under which their ancestors had lain for countless generations. Besides, the Germans had traditionally looked down on the Poles. And it did not take a sage to realize that Germany had, even in defeat, a rosier economic future than Poland. What jobs could Poland offer them, with little industry and still slimmer markets? To what advancement could a German youth aspire within the Polish state? The answer was obvious. Too few jobs and too little hope. Yet Poland insisted and in her insistence absorbed one million Germans, Germans who for the most part would look to Berlin rather than to Warsaw for aid and solace.

Yet what choice did Poland have? In the east it needed non-Polish territories as a buffer to absorb the impact of a

Russian attack before it reached Poland proper. This buffer, it was hoped, would buy Poland time to arm and garrison its strongholds.

The Allies—led by Britain, France, and America—favored this, for they recognized that the brave Poles would, in their stand, give the west a chance to rearm itself, as well. Particularly then, because of the Communist Revolution, Russia was viewed with great mistrust. Indeed, the entire French foreign policy in the east was literally to create a buffer zone formed by the small nations of the area. This "Cordon Sanitaire," or sanitary barrier, was designed to keep away both the germs of Bolshevism and the westward hunger of the Russians. So in this regard the Polish dreamers and western realists were in full accord.

As everyone—Poles and Allied statesmen alike—reasoned, to be a viable nation Poland would need industry and production. The elements of economic stability were concentrated in the west, in the newly acquired, Germanic lands in West Prussia, Posen, and Pomerania, lands that when ceded would become known as the Polish Corridor. Danzig, a thoroughly German city, was declared a "Free City" under League of Nations mandate to serve as Poland's only port.

From a Polish point of view, this was simply just retribution. The Allied motives, however, were not wholly altruistic. The move would weaken Germany both economically and politically, for with the lost factories and population also went the contiguousness of the German nation. East Prussia became a Teutonic island in a sea of Slavic and Baltic lands.

Germany, of course, was infuriated. Not only had Prussia, the jewel of the empire, been dismembered, but also the beneficiaries of that act were the despised Poles. The loss of the Corridor and Danzig would go far to ensure that the ancient enmity of Germans for Poles continued unabated.

Throughout her history Poland has repeatedly risen on the strength of one single man, seldom on the strength of any institutions she had created—a factor that, in the eyes of

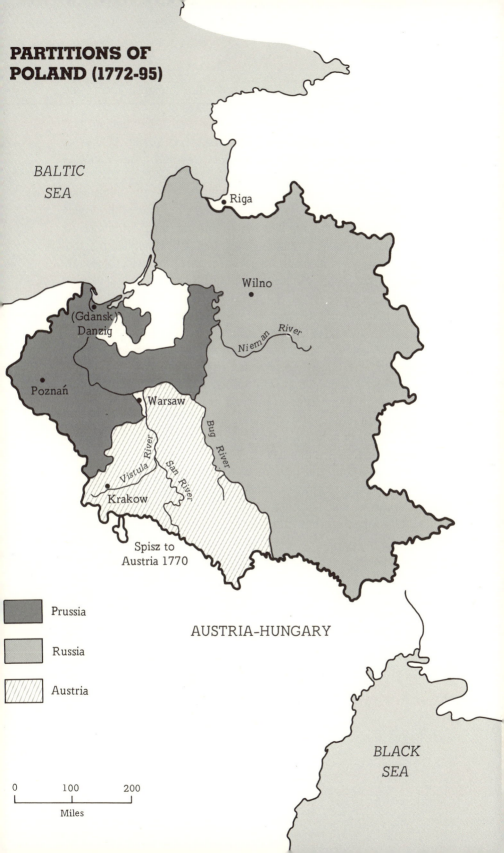

# PARTITIONS OF POLAND (1772-95)

BALTIC
SEA

• Riga

• Wilno

(Gdansk)
Danzig

*Nieman River*

• Poznań

Warsaw

*Vistula River*

*San River*

*Bug River*

• Krakow

Spisz to
Austria 1770

AUSTRIA-HUNGARY

BLACK
SEA

Prussia

Russia

Austria

0     100     200

Miles

many, has contributed heavily to her unhappy past. The experience of 1918 would be no different.

Just before the onset of the war, Polish nationalism had been personified by Jozef Pilsudski and Roman Dmowski, both genuine patriots, both deeply devoted to the cause of Poland, but sharing very little else.

Born to a noble family in Lithuania in 1857, Pilsudski embodied many of the problems and promises of the Polish nation. His birthplace was Wilno, the capital of Lithuania. As part of the Polish-Lithuanian kingdom, Wilno had seen a constant influx of Poles and now was largely inhabited by people of Polish descent. He grew up under Russian domination, and at school, as he recalled, his Russian teachers' purpose was to "crush the dignity and independence of their Polish and Lithuanian students, to minimize or deny Polish accomplishments and to laud Russian victories at the expense of Poland." To object would mean expulsion and with it a "wolf ticket"—a record that would deny the offender further education with the Russian empire. Holding himself in control, Pilsudski managed to graduate and to go to Kharkov, in Russia, to study medicine. There he became known to the police as a political troublemaker. When the opportunity arose to implicate him in a bizarre plot to assassinate the czar, they jumped at the chance. Arresting him under this pretext, even though he had not been involved, they quickly packed him off to Siberia, where he was to spend five long years. After

*Jozef Pilsudski, shown here as a young man, rallied Polish nationalists in the Russo-Polish War in 1920, and led his country until 1935.*

serving his time, he returned to Wilno where, to further the cause of Polish nationalism, he published a Socialist underground newspaper.

This time it took the Russian secret police eight years to catch up to him. Not unexpectedly, he was jailed again. At first he was kept in a maximum security cell in Warsaw, from which he managed to smuggle messages to the leadership of the Polish Socialist Party (PSP). Ostensibly driven mad by his imprisonment, he was transferred to an insane asylum in the Russian city of St. Petersburg (today's Leningrad). From there, where security was not so tight, he escaped a few months later to reappear perfectly sane in Galicia, a part of Poland under Austro-Hungarian rule. His "madness" had been a total sham. The story of how he had tricked and made fools of the Russians quickly spread through all parts of Poland, making him something of an instant hero. In Galicia he resumed his Socialist ties and activities but without involving himself in the philosophical aspects of the party. He was not in search of a doctrine. His goal was simple and clear. He wanted Polish freedom, and the PSP seemed the most likely vehicle to get him to his objective. Realizing that he would be more useful in a practical rather than theoretical position, the party put him in command of its fledgling terrorist organization. Concentrating his efforts solely on Russian Poland, Pilsudski went to work. Happily freeing political prisoners, holding up bank couriers, and robbing Russian army paymasters, he created for himself a Polish Robin Hood image. These efforts were to be crowned with a daring train robbery, which would bankroll his next and more ambitious project: the creation of a nucleus for a Polish national army.

In all his activities, Pilsudski had been careful not to threaten the Austro-Hungarian authorities. After all, he needed their territory for a safe base. So when the Austrians saw bands of Polish men taking up riflery and basic infantry drills, and not acting in any seditious ways they gladly helped them by supplying obsolete Austrian army rifles and letting them use their own parade grounds. Before long these small bands began to number not dozens but hundreds of men.

By 1914 the clouds of global war were gathering and Pilsudski's dream of the destruction of all three of Poland's occupiers was on its way to being turned into reality by World War I.

Pilsudski recognized Russia as the greatest threat to Poland, so when war broke out, his first act was to offer the Austro-Hungarian empire the Polish Legion, with himself as leader as an invasion force against Russia.

Born in 1864, Roman Dmowski was in many ways the antithesis of Pilsudski. While Pilsudski favored action, Dmowski was a man of thought. While Pilsudski did not question Poland, Dmowski asked himself *what is* Poland. And most importantly, while Pilsudski could only envision an independent nation, Dmowski favored a semi-autonomous status, one that would keep Poland an integral part of Mother Russia.

The son of a successful contractor, Dmowski was, like Pilsudski and many of their contemporaries in the last quarter of the nineteenth century, deeply involved in politics during his university years. But his activism led him into conflict with the Russian police, and he was forced to flee first to France and then to Austrian Poland. His ideological bent led him in 1897 to become a founder of the National Democratic Party (NDP), a party whose basic tenet was finding an accommodation with, rather than the overthrow of, the present imperial regimes. The NDP viewed this attitude as a realistic appraisal of the conditions, and they may well have been right. In their zeal to be practical, they came to the conclusion that the only feasible Poland would be one belonging to either Germany or Russia, with Russia being the least distasteful of the two. That this approach was essentially foreign to the Polish temperment was something that the NDP overlooked and something that undoubtedly contributed greatly to Pilsudski's supremacy when the allied victory in World War I opened the way for a reborn Polish nation. Thus it was not surprising that at the end of the war Dmowski would head for France to look after Polish interests and Pilsudski would march to Warsaw to organize the Second Polish Republic.

The years from 1918 to 1919 were very good for the Poles. First, nearly all of their territorial demands had been met even though vaguely, for most of Poland's frontiers had been left ill-defined. Then the repatriated Polish Legions had come home strong enough to subdue those nationalistic movements within the ethnic minorities that opposed Warsaw rule. And the country was sighing in relief as recognition of Pilsudski's obvious ability and leadership reassured them that there *was* a direction and a firm hand at the top, since these factors were recognized as having a major impact in Polish politics.

Even before making sure that the internal questions were settled, Pilsudski tackled what he saw as the most important issue: the strengthening of Poland. His basic belief—one shared by all Poles—was that Polish survival as an independent nation depended mostly on a militarily strong Poland. To this end he embarked on a series of aggressive steps against most of its neighbors. These attacks had as their basic purpose to swiftly acquire new territories as buffer lands and to keep actual and potential enemies off balance. That this would prevent any of these countries—Czechoslovakia, Germany, Russia, Lithuania, and Rumania—from ever trusting Poland seemed at the moment unimportant. The paramount issue for Poland was to ensure the creation of a state powerful enough to deter attack either from Germany or from Russia. That in the end Poland would be cornered by *both* of them acting in unholy concert may be one of history's most tragic ironies. That event, however, was still over twenty years away.

One of Pilsudski's first acts as Chief Marshal had been to offer free repatriation and safe conduct to the eighty thousand German troops still occupying Poland. His only condition: leave all your weapons behind. The Germans happily complied, their only interests being to leave the wretched country where so many of them had died and to be demobilized. Shortly after that fifty thousand superbly equipped and seasoned Polish veterans were repatriated from France and arrived to bolster Poland's hopes.

With the Germans gone, but with their equipment now in Polish hands, Pilsudski decided on a bold step: attack Russia before it could recover from its defeat at the hands of the Germans and from the devastations of her civil war.

Russia, an ally of France and England, had toward the end of the war been defeated and was forced by the Germans to sue for a separate peace. This was not surprising, for the Russian troops at the front were both ill-equipped and thoroughly demoralized by the news of the revolutions at home. After much bloodshed, these revolutions eventually created the communist state known as the Union of Soviet Socialist Republics—the Soviet Union—with Vladimir I. Lenin as its leader. In the meantime, civil war reigned supreme in Russia, pitting the Communist Red army against the so-called White Russian army, which was loyal to the old regime. Contingents from a number of countries including the United States fought the communists in Russia. But these foreign troops were few in number; the largest, the Czech Legion, numbered only twenty thousand men. Pilsudski attempted to recruit allies. No other nation would join him in what they saw as a suicidal venture. Even in defeat Russia loomed too large and powerful for most of the other countries.

Poland, going it alone, invaded Russia on April 25, 1920, capturing Kiev two weeks later. The fall of Kiev, the capital of the Ukraine and once the capital of ancient Russia, seemed a decisive victory. But the resilience of Russia had not been anticipated. Shortly after, a cossack army, which had last been seen a thousand miles away, whirled in out of the east and broke through the Polish lines. Other Soviet armies followed. Stunned, the Poles were forced to retreat to the very gates of Warsaw itself. There, while her envoys in Russia and in France were pleading for lenient peace terms, Pilsudski in a series of brilliant maneuvers split and enveloped the Russian armies to the astonishment of all of Europe, which was daily awaiting news of the fall of Warsaw, and with it the death of Poland. Then the news arrived: the Russians were fleeing. Not just stopped, or retreating, but fleeing, with the victorious Poles in hot pursuit. No one in any capital, besieged Warsaw included, could believe this. But it was true. And as the bells rang joyously throughout Poland, entire Russian divisions were surrendering to the Poles. Pilsudski had done it. And in what was to be the last great cavalry charge, the Soviet cossack army was annihilated by massed Polish troops inside a narrow valley. Glory had returned to Poland. In a matter of two days, Pilsudski had turned what had seemed a certain Soviet victory into a shameful rout.

Once again, the Poles had done the incredible. They had faced half of the sixteen armies the Reds commanded and had defeated them all. Not only that. Lenin, who had envisioned cheering Polish peasants welcoming his troops and joining their ranks, was sorely disappointed. Perhaps because Polish rule was still so new, perhaps for other reasons, even the inhabitants of what had been Russian territory viewed the Red soldiers with suspicion and outright hostility.

The resulting Peace of Riga gave Poland additional Russian lands. Yet in the long run this would prove to be a Pyrrhic, or hollow, victory for the Poles, for the territories they conquered would, by Polish mismanagement, come to be a huge burden instead of the envisioned asset.

In the west, meanwhile, problems with the Germans over the province of Upper Silesia had not only arisen but had also brought about pitched battles between Polish "volunteers" and Freikorps units. Although the former were basically civilians in paramilitary formations, the latter were seasoned German veterans aligned in private armies, which were secretly subsidized by Berlin. Silesia was a rich region whose population was predominantly German, yet whose incorporation into Poland was essential to the viability of a Polish state. The allies decided to partition it, awarding two thirds to Germany. Although on a territorial basis this seemed to favor the

Germans, the Poles got 40 percent of the population and most of the mines and heavy industry in the area. The Germans accepted the settlement most grudgingly, feeling that this was one more Polish insult to be paid back later. Thus Poland in less than two years managed to guarantee itself the enmity of not only most of her small neighbors but also of Germany and Russia.

Poland's only access to the sea was through the Free City of Danzig. When sorely needed French munitions for the Russo-Polish War arrived, German dockworkers in Danzig refused to unload them. When they were sent overland, the Germans turned them back at the French border. The Czechs, too, denied them passage.

The only solution was to have an exclusively Polish port. To this end the sleepy fishing town of Gdynia, some ten miles north of Danzig, was to be transformed. In 1920 work began on the port facilities, and in the astonishingly short span of fifteen years, it became one of the major ports of the world, surpassing Danzig, its next door rival, and nearly collapsing its economy. The Danzigers would not forget that.

With Marshal Pilsudski the undisputed ruler of Poland, the task of reconstruction was undertaken. In what had been a devastated country where starvation had raised its spectral face, industry and agriculture now thrived. True the worldwide depression of the 1930s was taking its toll in Poland, too. But the Polish currency, the zloty, was stabilized after a wobbly beginning and Poland prospered. Much of Poland's success was due to massive aid provided by France and the United States, plus the huge efforts of the Polish population in America. Had these good works been spent evenly and freely throughout the country, perhaps some of the separatist sentiments in Poland's minorities might have been dissipated. As it was, the eastern territories of Byelorussia and the Polish Ukraine, where the need was greatest, were neglected as they had always been.

With French assistance the might of the Polish forces grew, even while absorbing an exorbitantly large part of the national budget. Universities, which had been closed, were reopened and thousands of new schools built.

In 1919 Pilsudski had offered to march to Moscow at the head of a million-man Polish army if the Allies would only pick up the tab. France and Britain had declined the offer. Others were not interested. Pulsudski got halfway there, anyway. Yet although his 1920 victory might discourage the Russians, he realized that Poland's only safety now lay in defensive alliances and nonaggression pacts. It is sad to say that these produced little more than employment for the diplomats involved. There were numerous treaties with the French, the Russians, the Germans, the Czechs, the Hungarians, and the British. Yet when push came to shove, no country, least of all Poland, responded to anything except her own needs. If those needs were in accord with a treaty, then well and good. If not, expediency—the highest authority—prevailed. In the United States it was realized that most of Europe was busily signing treaties that would often put a nation on *both* sides of a quarrel. For Americans who had left the Continent convinced that they had fought the war to end all wars, this showed them a Europe where hypocrisy and cynicism were rampant. Wanting none of it, they turned their backs and embarked on an isolationist policy.

In the late twenties Pilsudski had laid down three basic rules that were to control Polish policy until World War II: (1) strengthen Poland's forces; (2) don't back down in the face of German threats; and (3) don't threaten Russia. Thus when opportunities were offered to join anti-Soviet alliances, the Poles always declined.

But regarding Germany, Pilsudski took a number of bold steps, challenging German might. They proved successful, even against Hitler.

But Pilsudski could not last forever. Ridden by cancer of the stomach, the marshal began to decline late in 1934, and on May 12, 1935, at the age of sixty-seven, Jozef Pilsudski, the Commander of the Polish Legions and First Marshal of Poland, died. He left a gap that no one was to fill.

Recognizing the stature of Pilsudski, one is tempted to speculate: would he have been able to save Poland from invasion in 1939? Most likely not. Germany and Russia moved then without regard to Poland's actions, and against their combined might the Poles would have still perished, regardless of their leadership. The only thing that could have saved Poland would have been concerted Anglo-French action, something the old marshal had long advocated but which, when it finally came, would arrive too late to save Poland.

For the next four years Poland was ruled to a large extent by the legacy of Pilsudski. Colonel Jozef Beck, who had been Pilsudski's foreign minister, would remain in this crucial post until 1939. Marshal Eduard Rydz-Smigly, Pilsudski's handpicked successor, would be appointed to the military posts held by his now dead chief.

One change would come about, however, and that was the advent of Colonel Adam Koc's Oxon movement. Patterned after the fascist model, it attempted to emulate the Nazi's anti-Semitic exploits, something Pilsudski had held in tight check. With Jews comprising 10 percent of the total population and over one third of Warsaw's people, this was a very real issue—an issue that under German control would in a few years transform the haven the ancient Polish kings had offered to European Jewry into one of the largest human slaughterhouses the world has known.

Through a number of incidents, Beck let the Germans know that Poland would resist and react violently if attacked. As long as Polish demands were supported by bigger guns, Hitler backed down. But after 1935 the new German army began to flex its considerable and fast-growing muscle. Polish stands were now seen in Berlin more and more as the barkings of a leashed dog, for Poland by itself ceased to be more than a substantial nuisance to Germany. The only real teeth she could bare were the hopes of French backing, and Paris by this time was making no secret of its dislike for Beck.

The French were faced with a dilemma. Much as they

were happy to see the Poles absorb the initial onslaught of a German attack, they did not want Poland to become so strong militarily as to be encouraged to make territorial incursions on her own. The object of such an attack would naturally be one of Poland's smaller neighbors, most of whom were allies of France. Therefore, France, Poland's principal arms supplier, kept the Polish arsenal limited to obsolete weapons—and small quantities even of those.

To make matters worse from a Polish point of view, France had begun to look upon Soviet Russia with considerably less fear. Thus Poland's dual shock absorber function—against Germany and Russia—was now less crucial as far as Russia was concerned. In addition, the French were seeing certain Polish moves as flirtations with Hitler, and the last thing they wanted was a French-financed Polish army reinforcing the German armed forces.

Even as late as 1939, the Poles were forcing Hitler to back down, principally over issues related to Danzig, the last one being an attempt by the German-controlled Danzig Senate to keep out the Polish customs inspectors, a move that the Poles successfully squashed. Unfortunately for the Poles, while these steps confirmed their backbone, they also made excellent material for Josef Goebbels, the Nazi's propaganda minister. He was to use the incidents with great skill to show the truculence of the Poles and the reasonableness of Germany. That often the Poles had been responding to deliberate German provocations was conveniently overlooked. Not satisfied with creating incidents, Goebbels was to increasingly improve on reality, culminating in 1939 with a wholly contrived Polish raid on a German village, a raid that would provide the ostensible provocation that would justify the long-planned German attack.

# CHAPTER III

# THE RISE
# OF THE
# THIRD REICH

**F**or a few years after World War I, Germany was a seething cauldron of conflicting and sometimes completely contradictory forces. Separatists called for individual components of the German empire to once again become separate nations, while Pan-Germanists argued that salvation was to be found in a monolithic Teutonic nation encompassing all Germans. The armed forces, that bastion of conservatism, were in places ruled by soldier and worker soviets, councils of enlisted men that were taking over the functions of the officer corps—yet these soviets would often take orders from the very men they had deposed. The Socialists, who were headed by President Friedrich Ebert, reluctantly ruled Germany and were secretly working to restore the monarchy that had recently been dethroned.

A few days before the Armistice of November 11, 1918, Germany had unwillingly become a republic. Unwillingly, because sentiment had been most strong for continuation of the empire. But President Wilson's message regarding ending the war had been unequivocal. If the Allies had to deal with "the military authorities and the Monarchical Autocrats of Germany . . . we must demand not negotiations for peace but surrender." So the kaiser quietly left for exile in

Holland a day after the republic had been declared, and a day before the Armistice itself.

The traditional forces that had kept the German empire together were coming unraveled. The kaiser, the army, the nobility, the very belief in "Deutschland über alles"—German supremacy—had all been eroded or crushed by World War I. This left confusion and bitterness as the unchallenged rulers of the nation.

To cap these misfortunes, in the spring of 1919, the terms of the Treaty of Versailles—as yet unsigned—were presented for acceptance to an exhausted and half-starved Germany. First, the treaty spoke of victors and vanquished, something that eluded large segments of the population to whom armistice meant just that—a cease-fire, not a surrender. The fact that economically and militarily the country was unable any longer to wage war was a fine point that would quickly be forgotten—forgotten even by those who had, in their search for a solution, created the very disturbances that were racking the country now.

After all, had not the fighting taken place on foreign soil—French, Belgian, Russian? Had not the returning troops parading fully armed in Berlin on December 1918 been greeted by President Ebert with "I salute you, who return unvanquished from the field of battle"?

What most Germans did not know or would not acknowledge, was that the country's industrial and economic base had been exhausted—that continuation of the war under these conditions would be tantamount to national suicide. In what proved to be only the first of a series of tragic mistakes, the Allies ignored the German perception of the Armistice.

So now, scarcely six months later, the Allies were proclaiming their conquest in the Treaty of Versailles. And proclaiming it unilaterally, for the Germans had not been consulted. The treaty terms demanded the handing over of hundreds of their most prominent men for trial and punishment as war criminals. The treaty also imposed demilitarization, the disarming of all but one hundred thousand men and the stationing of Allied troops on German soil. Germany's overseas possessions were to be distributed amongst the Allies. From Germany, itself, huge chunks were to be carved out. Alsace-Lorraine, that German-speaking French region would, after fifty years of German control, be repatriated. Czechoslovakia and much of Poland were to be hacked out from both Germanic empires, while smaller pieces were to go to Belgium and Denmark.

And then came the bill from the Reparations Commission: five billion dollars immediately—in coal, timber, food, factories—and more to be determined later. Feeling that Germany was responsible, the Allies were asking it to foot the bill for the whole war.

What had happened then to Wilson's Fourteen Points upon which a just peace and a brave new world were to be founded? Simply, that the Allies, particularly the French, had nearly been brought to their own knees before the infusion of American men and arms and money turned the tide. Remembering the fear and despair of those days, the Allies were determined to seek vengeance, retribution, and safety. The only way to achieve these aims, they felt, was to weaken Germany so much that it would not again be able to wage war.

So the French first, then the English, forgot Wilson's lofty words and meted out their harsh dictates in the belief that only buttressed by them could the Allies, Europe, and the world, sleep peacefully.

To the Germans an ultimatum was delivered on June 16: sign by June 28, or we will march again.

The German nation cried out in anguish, writhed in pain, but accepted the terms. Under her breath, though, she swore revenge for the humiliation and the injustice it was being forced to bear. There was nothing else that Germany could do now. But a day would come when it would no longer find this true. A day when strength would return, and it was for that day that Germany would live. But for now, she stood disheveled, impoverished, and most of all, leaderless. Germany's eyes, though, were wide open, and in her anger she

*The people of Berlin line up for hot soup*
*at a street stand run by the Salvation Army*
*during the dark days following World War I.*

stood ready to blindly give her all to the man who could offer to give back the dignity and pride the treaty had so harshly stripped. Behind this man Germany would march some day. The Germans were not the only ones to see this. Ferdinand Foch, the French marshal, upon reading the terms, had said with sorrow, "This will not bring peace, only a twenty year Armistice." His prediction would fall short by only a few months.

The treaty literally flattened Germany, presumably achieving its objective. Unhappily it also created the issue and the climate that would both unite the German people and blunt their judgment enough that they could become willing followers of a man like Adolf Hitler.

Meanwhile, the Roaring Twenties were anything but jolly in Germany. Because of reparation payments and internal disorder, the German mark kept losing its value. At first the decline of the mark was not so fast. Last week's salary might only be worth half as much as it had been the year before. But then it came down faster and faster. Eventually, a week's pay would buy a pair of shoes. Half a year later the same pair would take a full month's earnings. Strikes and marches were daily occurrences. So wages went up. Then prices. Then wages. Then prices, in an endless, ever accelerating spiral until no one held money for more than a few minutes. It would take a wheelbarrow load of marks to buy a loaf of bread. A lifetime's savings would be required to pay for a single meal. In November 1923 the mark, which normally had traded at four marks to one dollar, would go at the rate of four billion marks to a single dollar. And it would get worse. Money ceased to have value, and barter became commonplace. But in the modern world, without money, there can be no commerce, so industry was nearly forced to come to a standstill. And more people lost their jobs.

Oswald Spengler, a German historian, had prophetically foreseen his country's future when he had written. "We must, like the French in 1793, [the period of the French Revolution] go through to the end in our misfortune. We need a chastisement compared to which the four years of the Great War are nothing . . . until we are brought to such a state of excitement and despair that a dictatorship resembling that of Napoleon will be regarded universally as a salvation." In Spengler's city of Munich such a man was rising.

Adolf Hitler had been born in Austria on April 20, 1889, the son of a minor customs officer, Alois Hitler, and his second cousin Klara Poeltzl. Hitler's early years were marked only by the frequent changes of school which the restless Alois' wanderings forced on him, and by the conflicts the young boy would have with what he was later to call his hard and domineering father. At the age of eleven he declared his decision to become an artist, an ambition that was only to be set aside when politics became his prime passion.

After a sojourn in Vienna, where he led a thoroughly Bohemian life, young Hitler moved to Munich, a city he quickly came to love. It was there that in 1914, when war broke out, that he joined the German army after the Austrians had turned him down as being unfit for duty. Hitler was to serve with considerable distinction, although strangely he only achieved the rank of corporal. He was twice wounded and several times decorated for bravery. He even earned the Iron Cross, First Class, a medal seldom awarded to an enlisted man. Toward the end of the war, Hitler was gassed by the English in Belgium and sent to recuperate in a hospital in Germany. Blind for several weeks as a result of the gas, he fully regained his eyesight only after the Armistice had begun and the Germany he so loved was crumbling.

Hitler had always hated Jews, feeling in his early Vienna days that the city was controlled by them. Later, on his return to Germany as a wounded soldier, he would say that in the cities he had visited there, every clerk he had seen was a Jew and every Jew a clerk. His anti-Semitism (like that of many other Germans) would soon equate Jew with Red when the communists nearly took over the German government at the end of the war. He saw both the Jew and the Red as being bent on destroying the kind of Germany that embodied all his dreams. Everywhere he turned, it seemed to him that the Communist leadership was Jewish, starting with Karl Marx and ending with the local luminaries. So, to the sorrow of millions of Jews, the twin specters of his fear were to be fused into an easily identified and much maligned race.

After the Armistice Hitler remained in the army, where his staunchly conservative views and his talents as a proselytizer were quickly recognized. Among his tasks was reporting on the goals of the endless number of political groups that kept sprouting. Such a group was the German Workers Party, which had been founded by one Anton Drexler, a Munich machinist. The "party," as Hitler would soon find out when he went to his first meeting, consisted of some one hundred members, of which only twenty or so were present. But Drexler's platform galvanized Hitler, for in it he saw crystallized much of his own thinking. Basically Drexler advocated a working class, nationalistic government. To Corporal Hitler, who had seen so much poverty in Vienna and the indifference of the middle class to it, this was a vital element. That the platform recognized the absolute need for a single German state, made it twice as appealing.

The next day, to his surprise, a postcard arrived. He had been accepted in the German Workers Party. At first he laughed, he remembered later, for he had not even applied. Besides he had wanted to found his own party. But Hitler met with the German Workers Party again, becoming the seventh member of its governing committee. Soon the group would expand to include Ernst Rohm, a homosexual bully, who headed the SA, the early Nazi storm troopers, until his execution by Hitler in 1934; Dietrich Eckart, a writer and poet, who would be called the spiritual father of National Socialism, a name the movement would soon acquire and shorten to Nazi; Alfred Rosenberg, the party's chief theoretician; Hermann Goering, a war hero, who had commanded Manfred von

Richthofen's squadron after the death of the famed "Red Baron." He was later to head the German air force, the Luftwaffe, and would later die as a war criminal. It was with men such as these that the nucleus of the Nazi party was founded.

Hitler was an able organizer and an excellent speaker. Soon his enormous abilities began to show, as the meetings moved from dingy taverns to huge halls. Now a different Hitler began to appear. The brave, decent soldier of the trenches, the Corporal Hitler who would share his all with his comrades and for whose life he would risk his own, began to fade. "Adi," the artist who had painted pictures for his fellow soldiers and who honored his flag above all, somehow ceased to exist. In his place rose an evil genius, but a genius nonetheless. This was the man behind whom the humiliated German nation would later unite, rally, and conquer. But where other conquerors had often left behind pieces of civilization and bits of culture, this man's passage would bequeath only misery, oppression, savagery, and senseless death. He would epitomize for us the dark side of our nature, man's inhumanity to man.

Perhaps the most tragic fact of all is that in his book *Mein Kampf* ("My Struggle"), Hitler faithfully spelled out the goals and methods he was to follow in the New Order—the New Order that he envisioned would rule a Nazi world. Hitler wrote *Mein Kampf* while serving a prison sentence for leading an unsuccessful revolt against the government of the Bavarian state in 1923. Even though Hitler's revolt failed, this event, which became known as the Beer Hall Putsch, catapulted him into national prominence and gave him a forum from which to bring new strength to his fledgling party.

Germany meanwhile was struggling mightily to remain a viable nation and a republic. For six years after 1923, the gods seemed, if not *actually* to smile at Germany, at least to have stopped frowning. Strict monetary measures were instituted, and these, together with American aid and German hard work, brought back sanity and hope. After a while, it seemed as though the republic might, in spite of all, be capable of surviving on German soil.

Then came the debacle of 1929: the Wall Street crash that was heard around the world. Its impact sent not only America but also many other nations into bouts of bleakness and despair. Germany was no exception. Unhappily for it, though, the situation was far worse. Its people had only known employment and security for such a brief time, and its leaders in those years had been trying to genuinely improve the lot of its working people. As such, all the trappings of a modern, caring state had been instituted, far ahead of most other corners of the globe. Unemployment insurance, pension plans, medical aid, all these costly programs were in place—in place, but unable to meet the urgent needs of millions suddenly unemployed. Soon, for the second time in little more than a decade, Germany was plunged into hopelessness. Perhaps by now the chastisement that Spengler had foreseen might be complete. Perhaps the dreaded redeemer he had described might now be near, if not at hand.

Ridiculed after the aborted Beer Hall Putsch of 1923, the Nazi party had receded from the public eye. Yet it had been quietly growing. From its membership of one hundred men in 1920, it had grown to twenty seven thousand in 1925, and by 1929, one hundred eighty thousand members were enrolled. Not only that but a busy Hitler had built the party into an organization that in effect duplicated the government. He had not said in vain that it was "not enough to overthrow a government, you must have a new government ready to take over from the one that has just failed." He had written that a few years earlier, when these had been but words on paper. Now in 1929 the structure called for in his book *Mein Kampf* had been brought into reality. It was a reality that would not yet come into service, for although Hitler thought he was ready for Germany, Germany was not yet ready for him. But the time was coming. Unemployment was growing. The roaring of the Reds was louder, the strikes and disorder more frequent. Hitler's storm troopers bullied the opposition, but

*Adolf Hitler speaks to a gathering of his*
*Nazi followers in the party's early days.*

other parties had their own organized thugs, too. President Paul von Hindenburg—the old marshal, the venerable father figure—was well past eighty, and what had been an iron will and a sharp mind, was now an old man drifting into dotage and senility. The handwriting was on the wall. The republic was collapsing, and Hitler's time was coming near. It finally arrived on January 30, 1933. On that day Hindenburg, now eighty-seven, named Hitler chancellor of Germany, a position similar to that of a prime minister. And it had been done quite democratically. The people after all had given Hitler and his party close to fourteen million votes. A far cry from the Munich days scarcely more than twelve years ago when a hundred names were all that he could muster. Yet for Hitler, the position of chancellor was not enough; his power was still limited. But soon the old marshal had to die, and Hitler pinned his hopes on that day. When it came, in a series of astonishing moves, he secured the loyalty of the army, thus eliminating the only rival that could thwart his dreams. The Wehrmacht (the armed forces) swore a new oath: "I swear by God this sacred oath that I will render unconditional obedience to Adolf Hitler, the Führer [leader] of the German Reich and Nation, the Supreme Commander of the Wehrmacht and that I shall be ready, as a brave soldier, to lay down my life at any time for this oath."

Total power was now his.

From this day on Germany moved with dizzying speed. Just like a giant sponge, the government absorbed the masses of unemployed. Some people were put to work in building highways—constructing the famous autobahns—others worked in factories, where export goods and armaments began to be produced. It was like a giant summer camp, except that work was being thrown in, a welcome thought for those who had for so long been idle. There were campfires and songs and games and uniforms. There was ample food and comradeship. Most of all there was a new sense—the sense of working for a common goal, a goal that was shared by nearly all.

The others—the dissenters, the doubters, all those who dared to question or oppose—would go to a different kind of camp, a camp where the only singing would be the wind through barbed wire, where the only things in ample supply were fear, brutality, and death.

Hitler had delivered. There was work for all. Now the next order of things was to restore German pride. To do so Hitler would have to rebuild the army and, at long last, put German soldiers on all of German soil. To this end he ordered the army to triple its strength by 1934, and to be prepared for conscription the following year. He then asked the General Staff, the controlling body of the German armed forces, for a plan to reoccupy the demilitarized Rhineland. Hermann Goering was set to work training pilots under the innocent banner of the League for Air Sports. The Treaty of Versailles had forbidden Germany to have any armaments, and so Hitler ordered submarines to be built secretly in Finland, Spain, and Holland, while artillery and tanks were being tested for him in Russia.

In his determination to rearm Germany, however, Hitler did not neglect the diplomatic front. For the next five years most of his international gains would be achieved through diplomatic skill and bluff, not force of arms.

The list of his gains was long. First in March 1935 he announced to the world what he had already ordered—universal conscription. The Allies officially protested, but otherwise did nothing.

He then unveiled the Luftwaffe in its new sky-blue uniforms. The treaty had forbidden the Germans to have an air force. France and England, desperate for peace, looked the other way.

Then Hitler raised the stakes. In open defiance of the Allies, he marched three battalions into the Rhineland, on March 7, 1936. The French and British, terrified of war, did nothing. The German General Staff was terrified, too. They knew they could not back up their bluff if the French reacted. German troops had secret orders. Retreat if opposed. After all, the planes of the fledgeling Luftwaffe were only trainers; all that the ground troops had were rifles and a few machine guns, nothing more. A determined French military police-man could have sent them back. But none showed up. Instead the people of the Rhineland welcomed the Wehrmacht sol-diers with flowers, kisses, and hurrahs. It was as if each marching man were a lost son or brother to each woman, man, or child in the cheering crowd. Hitler had once more delivered.

The French had second thoughts but would not move without the British. London, safe behind the English Channel, would not fight. After all, the British said, the Germans were only going into their own back garden.

Soon they would find out that Hitler had further planting plans.

# CHAPTER IV

# DAYS OF APPEASEMENT: 1937-1939

**N**ineteen thirty-seven was to be a strange year. With the remilitarization of the Rhineland, the French realized that the buffer strip they had fought for to keep the Germans at bay was gone. The only defenses they had left now were the presumably impregnable fortifications that comprise the Maginot Line and a fast-fading reputation as the finest army in the world. The Belgians, upon seeing the lack of French spine, declined French assistance and decided to go it on their own, a decision that was to have tragic consequences in a brief time. The English heard the voice of Winston Churchill call out for more planes and grudgingly put the Hurricane fighters in production. Across the sea, however, America retreated further into its isolationist shell. And Japan, that distant empire, had its Manchurian conquest to digest, while its armies relentlessly chewed up a weak and strife-torn China.

In Russia Stalin feared internal threats against his regime and was purging the country of his real and imagined enemies. The death count by 1937 was in excess of three million and still rising.

In Spain civil war rent the country. On one side were the Nationalists, who supported the establishment roles of government and the Church. On the other were the Republicans, anarchists, and idealists of various stripes, who sought to change the ancient structures that had dominated Spanish life. In pursuit of their objectives, Spaniards turned to savagely killing each other with ample help from the outside world. To assist the Nationalist leader General Francisco Franco, the Italian dictator Benito Mussolini dispatched fifty thousand Fascist soldiers. But these men saw no reason they should get killed in a fratricidal war where they had no stake. So although they were willing to parade and march a lot, they sensibly did their best to avoid actual conflict. The Germans, who also supported the Nationalists, formed the Condor Legion. It provided air transport for Franco's troops and bombed his enemies, reporting the results to a learning Goering. On the other side, volunteers flocked to the cause of Republican Spain. International brigades were formed made up of Britons, Frenchmen, Canadians, Americans, Germans, Bolivians. Nearly every country and every shade of liberal and leftist opinion were represented, for many saw this as a philosophical war of oppression versus liberty. The Soviets helped the Republican's side with troops and arms, and when the war was lost to them in 1939, they quietly took the gold from Spain's treasury for "safekeeping," gold that is in Moscow to this day. In search of victory, justice, and order, the Nationalists bombed Guernica and marched communists in front of firing squads. In the name of liberty and equality, the Republicans burned churches and machine gunned convents filled with nuns, soldiers, and civilians.

Yet in spite of all of this, much of Europe was in a state of euphoria. Nations knew that war was near and inevitable, yet they clung tenaciously to little more than the hope that by wishing it away, war would go away. In England Neville Chamberlain was elected prime minister, accurately reflecting the prevailing mood of his own time. Chamberlain had been serving his government for some fifteen years. From that vantage point, he had watched the disintegration of France and had seen her value as a partner diminish. The alliance with the French made him uncomfortable. Dealing with them had always been frustrating because of France's lack of political stability. So this year, as the new prime minister, he would try a new tack. To this end he sought out Hitler to win Germany's friendship and confidence and thus to forestall the impending war. After all, he reasoned, what better way to disarm your enemy than by reaching out and taking its hand. In addition, many Britons secretly felt that the Treaty of Versailles had been too harsh on the Germans and that many of the steps undertaken by Hitler were, in fact, justified. At the same time, Britain's financial stability depended on concentrating its forces on the far-flung reaches of the empire, so peace in Europe, at almost any price, was recognized as essential.

Unfortunately, like other leaders, Chamberlain had failed to read *Mein Kampf.* Had he done so, he would have realiuzed that his approach to the Führer was precisely what Hitler wanted. When it came, it confirmed what Hitler had long suspected. The British would not fight; Hitler was safe. And since the French were not about to move without Britain, their ally, then France could be ruled out too. The rest of the world did not really matter. America was too far away; Soviet Russia seemed impotent; Japan was Germany's ally; and the other nations were too small and weak.

So Case Green, the code name for the plan of invasion of Czechoslovakia, was drawn up in June 1937. Under it, German troops would move on October 1, 1938. Meantime, Hitler signed an agreement with Poland regarding the treatment of each other's minorities. To seal the deal Hitler had twice remarked that Danzig "was bound to Poland." And to make sure the Poles got the message, he informed the Yugoslav prime minister that "While Danzig's status was a hard pill for Germany to swallow, it had to be accepted."

Few words could have been spoken with less sincerity. The whole issue of the Polish Corridor and Danzig's return to the Reich had been central to Hitler's "Reunification of all

Germans" plan. Danzig's and the Corridor's surrender to Poland at the end of World War I had been cause for much bitterness in Germany. Since Poland, to be viable, had to have a port, Danzig—an overwhelmingly German city—was separated from the Reich and put under the control of the League of Nations for the benefit of Poland. These moves had literally split Germany in two, leaving East Prussia a Teutonic island in a Baltic and Slavic sea. (Farther east, in Lithuania, Memel, too, was a Germanic city. In time, that was also to become part of the Third Reich.)

Again Hitler had been clear. Years earlier he had declared his ambition to unite all Germans under one flag. Together they would form the *Herrenrasse*, the master race.

In the Rhineland Hitler *had* been marching into his own back garden, and there it had been a very clear case of the master of the house returning home. Austria was to be his next step. Here, though, the issue would not be quite so clear.

When the Austro-Hungarian empire had been broken up in 1918, the sentiment for *Anschluss*, the union with Germany of the Germanic-Austrian sector, had been widespread and clear. However, both the French and the Italians, feeling that such a move would constitute a threat to their security, had vetoed the idea.

Only a few years earlier the Germanic Austrians had been the governing and business elite of a polyglot empire whose ethnic diversity surely must have made Wilson's head spin. For the president had envisioned a Europe where English would live in England, French in France, and Spaniards in Spain. However, eastern and central Europe were quite different and would not fit into this mold. The Austro-Hungarian empire was a prime example. Ten national groups constituted it: Austrians, Hungarians, Poles, Czechs, Slovaks, Ukranians, Rumanians, Croats, Slovenes, and Serbians. Although each had nationalistic tendencies, for the most part they were kept under control by a tolerant and reasonably just central government in Vienna. This empire, by Allied edict in November of 1918, ceased to exist. The empire with its fifty million souls was carved up into its ostensibly ethnic components. But the borders of the newly created states were quickly "adapted" as economic necessity and political viability transcended ethnic lines. Thus the Czechs annexed the Slovaks and swallowed three million Germanic Austrians in the Sudetenland. The Poles, in retaking Galicia, "assimilated" a part of the Ukraine, while in the west they took on quite a few Germans of their own. Their example was followed by all the new nations carved out from the old Austro-Hungarian empire. As a result, each wound up with sizable minorities of its neighbor's ethnic group. Hitler would fully exploit this feature later on.

Although the other former nations of the empire were viewed as friends, Germanic Austria and its six and a half million people were seen as foes by the victorious Allies. Thus it was not unnatural for the Austrians to see union with Germany as a desirable goal. However, Hitler's Reich was not what they had had in mind.

And so while the dream of a Pan Germanic nation beat in Austrian hearts, they kept on rebuffing Nazi advances.

Hitler stubbornly kept sending out feelers to see who would oppose *Anschluss.* Italy, which had once been afraid of the idea, would now, under Mussolini, not complain. France, as before, was too torn up by dissension to seriously object, let alone wage war over the issue. The British, under Chamberlain, had earlier offered to send their foreign minister to Berlin for talks. London was then apprised of Hitler's plans. Instead of protesting, London plaintively asked if the visitor would still be welcome. The Germans, greatly relieved, graciously answered that, of course, it would be so.

Feeling secure on all fronts, the Führer summoned the Austrian chancellor, Kurt von Schuschnigg, to Berchtesgaden (Hitler's mountain headquarters), and informed him of his terms. Simply put, they spelled the end of Austrian independence. Not only that, the Austrian was given but a few days to sign. On February 18, 1938, six days later, von Schuschnigg agreed to Hitler's terms. By this move, he tried to buy time, time to hold a plebiscite, to let the Austrian people by direct vote choose whether to remain independent or to join Hitler's Third Reich. The plebiscite was to be held on March 13, four days from the date when Schuschnigg announced it. This took the Germans by surprise. Even though sentiment for *Anschluss* was strong, a plebiscite could go either way. Determined to stop it, Hitler ordered the Wehrmacht to march. They had to be in Vienna by Saturday, the day before the plebiscite.

To legalize his move Hitler had Arthur Seyss-Inquart, the newly appointed Austrian minister of the interior and a fervent Nazi, send a telegram to Berlin: "To reestablish peace and order and to prevent bloodshed . . . the provisional Austrian government asks the Reich to send German troops as fast as possible."

Hitler obliged, and one hundred thousand Wehrmacht soldiers marched into welcoming crowds everywhere. Since some seventy thousand Austrians were quickly arrested by Heinrich Himmler's secret police the Gestapo, that meant that only thirty thousand new beds needed to be found for the occupying forces. Austria was now part of the Third Reich.

Much of the world sighed with relief. The other German shoe had finally fallen, they thought, and there had not been war. Hitler, beside himself with joy, took care to announce to

*A triumphant Hitler is led to Vienna's Town Hall by the city's Lord Mayor after* Anschluss.

the world that all his territorial claims were now satisfied, an assurance that he had Goering personally extend to a somewhat skeptical Czech ambassador in Berlin.

That Czechoslovakia would be Hitler's next stop was a foregone conclusion. And the roots of this move, too, went back to World War I. At that time, to make Czechoslovakia a viable nation, the ancient states of Bohemia and Moravia as well as Slovakia were detached from defeated Austria. The problem was that most of southern Bohemia was not Czech or Slavic at all. This region, known as the Sudetenland, was peopled by three million Germanic Austrians who, in the way of all the central and eastern European states, would be viewed and treated as a suspect minority by the Czech government in Prague. Hitler found fertile soil there for his Pan-German views, and a strong Sudeten Nazi party under Berlin control was founded.

With Austria now a part of the German Reich, it was only logical that the Sudetenland should wish to join its Teutonic brethren. What is fantastic is that the French would for an instant even consider losing Czechoslovakia's huge defenses. The Czechs, unlike the Poles, had strong natural barriers along their German frontier, defenses they had taken good care to reinforce. In fact, the Wehrmacht had calculated that it would take about fifty divisions to storm them by frontal attack. In addition—again unlike the Poles—they had a good industrial base, and in their midst stood both the Skoda and Brno works, after Krupp the most formidable arms factories in Europe. To man and protect all this they had thirty-five well-trained superbly equipped divisions.

The Poles, like the French, however, were blind. All they could see was that with the dismemberment of Czechoslovakia they could help themselves to Teschen, a disputed Czech area. They failed to see that an independent Czech state would have strongly protected their southern flank and kept the so-called Moravian Gate closed as an avenue for

German invasion.

In May 1938 the Czechs, alarmed by German troop movements, ordered partial mobilization. At the same time Britain and France, alerted by the Czech reports, issued a warning to Hitler, a warning that Soviet Russia backed with threat of arms.

It sounded most impressive, but neither the French nor the British had their hearts in it. And Soviet assistance would be worthless unless Poland and Rumania permitted Red troops to pass through their territory, something both flatly refused to do. Besides, it was a false alarm. Hitler was not yet ready to move.

However, through its native Nazi party, the Sudetenland was kept in a state of high ferment, and Czech troops had to be brought in to quell sporadic rebellions. Summer passed. Then, on a glorious September day, an editorial in the London *Times* suggested that "the Czechs would be better off without the Sudetenland, since then they would be more homogeneous." By a strange coincidence, on September 15, one week later, Chamberlain flew to Germany, his first time on a plane, to inform Hitler that he had no objection to Sudeten self-determination. To make the meeting more cordial, they both made sure no Czech was present. A happy Hitler laid down his terms. Germany would take the Sudetenland; in return, Hitler would not declare war. Pleased, Chamberlain returned to London, where he invited the French to discuss the proposal. Again, no Czech was present. Once in accord, they *informed* the Czechs of their decision. Give the Sudetenland away. Stunned, the Czechs—who believed that their French allies would back *them* and that the British would back the French, forcing Hitler to back down—moaned in despair, but in the end they agreed. Jubilant, Chamberlain on September 22 flew to the Rhine and gave Hitler his report. The Czechs had accepted the Führer's terms. There would be no war. To Chamberlain's astonishment Hitler said it was

*Britain's Prime Minister Neville Chamberlain
(left) meets with Hitler at Berchtesgaden in 1938
to discuss the fate of Czechoslovakia. At right
is the German foreign minister, Joachim von
Ribbentrop and, behind him, the British ambassador
to Berlin, Sir Neville Henderson.*

now too late: he had a new plan. The Czechs had five days to completely evacuate the Sudetenland before the German army moved in. No talk now of plebiscites or other alternatives. As a sop to Chamberlain, Hitler magnanimously gave the Czechs two more days. The new date was October 1, the Führer's own X Day for Case Green.

Meantime, the Czechs had mobilized. But Hitler was clever. He had enlisted Polish and Hungarian help in the dismemberment of Czechoslovakia and both obliged. The Poles now delivered *their* ultimatum to the Czechs. But things began to go wrong. Hungary, poised to move, was stopped by Yugoslavia and Rumania, which had declared that they would march if Hungary attacked Czechoslovakia. The French ordered partial mobilization. Mussolini suggested a conference with Britain, France, Italy, and Germany to decide the issue. They all accepted. They would meet in Munich the following day. Naturally, no Czechs or dogs allowed. At the meeting the French and British tried to outbid each other in keeping the Führer happy. In the meantime, they went so far as to tell the Czechs that even if they should go to war and win, the Allies would still insist that the Sudetenland be German.

Beaten, the Czechs surrendered. And on October 1, right on schedule, the German army made its triumphal entry into the Sudetenland.

On the same day, in London, a tired Chamberlain smiled to a happy crowd that had just treated him to a rousing round of "For he's a jolly good fellow." From the first floor window of his residence at Number 10 Downing Street, he announced, "This is the second time that there has come back from Germany to Downing Street peace with honor. I believe it is peace for our time."

Few statesmen have been more wrong in their predictions.

Six months later, on March 15, Hitler swallowed the rest of Czechoslovakia.

Now Poland's turn had come.

■ 65 ■

CHAPTER

PRELUDE
TO WAR:
1939

**O**n April 3, 1939, scarcely two weeks after the elimination of Czechoslovakia as a country, the file on Case White was started. Its aims, bluntly stated in a directive from Hitler, were simple: destroy Poland. The destruction of Poland would eliminate the twin thorns of Danzig and Corridor. The Führer asked for full plans to be delivered to him in one month and implementation to be ready four months later. Thus September 1 became the invasion date, a date that, as with X Day for Case Green—the Sudetenland—Hitler would keep.

What Hitler did on that clear spring day was merely to establish parameters for an objective that had long existed. In a very real way Case White was born in 1919, on the day the Treaty of Versailles' terms were announced to a stunned German nation. Of these, none had rankled so much as the creation of the Polish Corridor and the loss of Danzig, that port so steeped in German tradition. That Danzig was a Free City under the League of Nations was of little import. That its existence had been dedicated to serving Poland filled German hearts with fury. Poland in its rebirth had mutilated Germany, for in creating the Corridor, East Prussia became separated from the Reich, and parts of West Prussia, Posen, and Pomerania were taken by the Poles. That many of these lands had for centuries been Polish until the partitions in the 1790s did not diminish German hatred. General Hans von Seeckt, the head of the German General Staff and the father of German rearmament, had expressed the country's and particularly the army's attitude: "The obliteration of Poland must be one of the fundamental goals of German Policy," so when the directive on Case White came through, it fell on enthusiastic ears, an enthusiasm that was made even more vivid by the brilliant successes of Hitler's bluffs in the Rhineland, Austria, and Czechoslovakia.

Up to this point, the generals had been appalled at the audacity the Führer had shown, for they recognized that Germany hadn't the military muscle to enforce her will if challenged. But each time the enemy had backed down, and Hitler had been proven right. By now, even the most timid men in the German General Staff had come to accept the accuracy of his judgment in such matters, and to limit themselves to the military questions within their own expertise. Thus Hitler's international successes firmly pushed the Wehrmacht back into its barracks and away from the political arena. Had the Allies called any of Germany's bluffs, Wehrmacht support might have been withdrawn, and without it Hitler could well have come tottering down.

But for the invasion of Poland to succeed the proper conditions had to be established. To that end Josef Goebbels, the Nazi minister of propaganda, was given free rein. Starting in May German newspapers began a barrage of accounts telling of atrocities the Poles were committing against the unarmed and defenseless Germans in the Corridor and in Danzig. At the same time Nazi organizations in those territories whipped up all manner of difficulties for the Poles. Drawing on the experience gained in Austria and the Sudetenland, new disruptive endeavors, new heights of seditious perfection were achieved.

On the diplomatic front Hitler's wily foreign minister, Joachim von Ribbentrop, began the alternating game of baring German teeth and dispensing false assurances. He masterfully played on the fragmentation of French politics to keep that country divided on the war issue. For the Right he presented Germany as a bulwark against Bolshevism; for the ruling Socialists he stressed the remoteness of Eastern Europe and the pointlessness of losing a single French franc or soldier there.

To the British Ribbentrop stressed their common Teutonic origins and the lack of German desire to challenge Britannia's rule over the waves, the unquestioned supremacy of the British navy. He also reminded Chamberlain that Germany was observing the terms of the Anglo-German Naval Pact of 1936. This pact, which only permitted German naval strength to be 35 percent that of Britain, incredibly left limitless the size of the Reich's land forces, a fact that could hardly reassure the French. That the chosen date to celebrate the treaty was the anniversary of Waterloo—the battle in which the combined German-British forces decisively defeated Napoleon—would be ominously noted by Paris.

However, in 1939 London had a nasty surprise for the Germans. Chamberlain, the appeasing Prime Minister who at Munich had acted as Hitler's lackey, had had enough. He at last realized that Hitler's objective was not just to unite under the Reich all the German peoples. He now recognized that Hitler's dreams went far beyond that goal, and that the Führer must be stopped lest England be destroyed. So on March 31 he announced a unilateral guarantee that committed Britain to go to war on Poland's side, were that country to be attacked. To emphasize the pact, peacetime conscription was begun in Britain for the first time. With these steps it seemed as though Hitler's effortless conquests would at last be checked.

To make matters worse for the Führer, the Russians began to worry for their own safety. Would Hitler stop with Poland? What about the ancient Germany policy of "Drang nach Osten," the "Drive to the East"? Was not *Lebensraum*, the living room Hitler sought for an expanding Germany, specifically to be found in Russia? With these thoughts in mind, Stalin pressed the democracies harder for a military agreement to contain Germany.

The Allies, feeling that dealing with the Soviets was distasteful and that the Russians had no other alternative anyway, literally sent their representatives on a slow boat to Russia. Further, although Stalin had asked that discussions be conducted at the highest level, the Allied representatives were second- and third-rank officers without any negotiating powers.

The Russians correctly interpreted this as little more than a patronizing gesture and began to pursue contact with the Germans in earnest. It would prove to be a decisive factor in starting World War II. Although Hitler hoped for Allied passivity, he did not in fact count on it seriously. He felt that the French army could easily be defeated and that the British would accept reasonable peace terms. But he did not want to contend with Russia until *he* had decided that the time had come. On Russia's side, there was method in Stalin's madness. If war came, he reasoned, the democracies and Germany would batter each other so severely that the victor would be weakened, if not easy, prey for the Red army.

But what of Poland? Ribbentrop had not neglected it. Earlier on, he had asked Colonel Jozef Beck, his Polish counterpart, to review "the urgent need to settle the Danzig question." Specifically he was asking for extraterritorial rights for a highway and railroad to unite the Reich with East Prussia, and for the return of the Free City to German control.

Beck's reply was firm: "Any attempt to incorporate the Free City into the Reich . . . must inevitably lead to conflict." He also reminded Ribbentrop that Hitler had recently and in the past given his assurances that he would not support any change in Danzig's status. Hitler, though, had served notice of his intentions in Poland, a fact that Beck quickly recognized.

Poland turned to France, which replied that she would honor her treaties. France offered some arms and had General Maxime Weygand, second in command of the French army, review the Polish army status. The general's conclusion "that nothing was lacking," must have filled Beck's mind with alarm since he well knew the condition of the Polish army. Beck then turned to the British who were at first quite cool. Had not Poland feasted on Czechoslovakia's body? But Chamberlain's moralistic tendency was overcome by a single fact. The loss of Poland would harm Britain. If Russia stood still, France and England would have to face the full impact of the Wehrmacht. So he offered Beck British backing.

The Pole could see, as Hitler had, that any Allied assistance would have to come by forcing Germany to fight on two fronts, east and west. He also could see that in the east, Poland would have to bear the full brunt. To that end Poland's effort must be to last long enough, to absorb the invasion impact for some days—two weeks or so at most—for the agreement with France specified that the French would march on the third day of war. Beck also knew, as did the Wehrmacht and the French, that the Siegfried Line, Germany's complex of fortifications facing the west was little more than a huge construction site at this time—certainly not a major obstacle for a concerted attack.

By now Beck had had several occasions to see the sorry effect of what temporizing to Hitler would bring. Being a proud and haughty man, he had no desire to join the ranks of other heads of state who had bowed to Hitler, including the Lithuanian premier, who had just handed over Memel, his country's only port. This Germanic enclave would be the last peaceful acquisition that a seasick but gloating Hitler would receive aboard the battleship *Deutschland,* steaming toward Memel for the anticipated welcoming reception.

On the home front, the Poles began to mobilize. One tends to think of Poland as a small country, yet in 1939 this was not so. In area it was about the same as Germany, with a population about two thirds that of France. If the French and Poles had joined, they could have fielded an army about the same size as the Third Reich's. By 1920 or even 1930 standards, the Polish contribution to its own defense would be a good one; therefore, General Weygand's appraisal that "nothing was lacking" in the Polish army was, in that light, not quite so off the mark. Technically and tactically, though, the Polish army was so far behind the Germans as to make the comparison utterly absurd. But the Poles did not know that. In fact, it would be three years before any country would field an army that could compare to the Wehrmacht.

Poland did not have any natural frontiers, and to make matters worse its industry, such as it was, was concentrated in the western half of the country, closest to Germany. Its transportation network could at best be described as seasonably passable—during the dry seasons. Here lay the Poles' one trump card: an attack on Poland, particularly by a mechanized army, *had* to come in summertime. And, the Poles thought, German mobilization for an invasion would take time. Again what they did not know was that under guise of summer maneuvers, the Wehrmacht had already been fully mobilized.

The Poles had counted on the September rains which would normally turn the country roads into mud ribbons and the shallow rivers into broad currents. Here, armor, tanks, personnel carriers, and motorized artillery would be useless and the horse invaluable. And Poland had the largest cavalry of any country. With muddy roads, they felt, Polish courage and strong horses would stop any invader. Everyone, including Hitler, recognized this. What Poland did not know was that the weather, like her other allies, would fail her, that the skies would not darken with rain until October, long after the Wehrmacht had begun to pull back, its job done. So much so that weeping Poles would wonder aloud if God had not in fact closed ranks with the Reich's battalions.

Meanwhile, in the summer of 1939, in Danzig and in the Corridor, the pressure grew. Goebbels' propaganda was having its effect. As Danzigers read German newspapers with accounts of "atrocities" committed by Poles, the local

*The Polish Cavalry, shown here during maneuvers, was the elite force of the Polish Army that mobilized in 1939.*

Nazi organizations waxed indignant. Torchlight parades, protest marches, and attacks on Jewish-owned stores were staged. This elicited harsh responses from the Polish police and the army, so escalation became inevitable. Thus fiction created friction, bringing about tragic results. In Germany itself, strangely enough, the press barrage failed to create the war hysteria that Hitler had hoped would justify his forthcoming acts. For Hitler was no longer concerned with Danzig or with the Corridor. It was no longer a question of returning ethnic Germans to the Reich. That stage had really been passed. Now what mattered was *Lebensraum*, making land available for Germans, land to guarantee self-sufficiency, first in foods, then in raw materials. And Poland had been earmarked as only the first step in that direction.

The Poles, however, were a proud and cocky people. The role that Hitler would have them assume was not in their plans, so they would fight. Too proud and too cocky, some would say, but what were their alternatives? After all, they thought, they were going into a war with Europe's largest army and navy at their side—France and England, both willing to march as soon as the alarum of invasion was sounded.

The tragedy that lurked had not as yet been unveiled. No one at that time had a true idea of the terrible efficiency of the Wehrmacht's tactics.

French tanks were bigger, better armed, and available in greater numbers. Britannia *did* rule the waves, and retaliation by France would force the Reich to fight a two-front war, the nemesis of German military thinking. Not only that, but with Britain joining the conflict, Germany would be blockaded and again, as in 1918, starved into submission. That the Wehrmacht could and would surmount all these obstacles was beyond the thinking of most German generals, never mind the British, French, or Polish.

The Poles in fact were more concerned with Russia as an enemy than with the Reich. After all, had they not denied the

Russians passage through their lands scarcely six months earlier? No, they knew that once on Polish soil, the Red army would like nothing better than to stay and become Poland's master. They feared Russian help more than German bayonets.

German investment in Poland had been substantial, and Poland's value as a market for German products was even greater.

This was not true of Russia. Poland *felt* itself to be part of the Western world, its very outpost, perhaps, but still a part of it. On the other hand, Russians and Poles were both Slavs one might argue. But the Poles traditionally had feared and disliked the Russians. So the Poles knew that in the end they would have to fight both Germans and Russians. But then their whole history had been caught up in that struggle. The only way that Poland had ever ceased to exist had been when Germans and Russians closed ranks. And that this could again occur in 1939 was laughable to Polish minds.

No, no sane man in Warsaw or for that matter in London, Paris, or Berlin would think such a thought. The British had been so very sure that Russia had no home other than with the Allies—so sure, in fact, that time and time again they had dealt with Russia as a third-rate power, leaving it outside the door to wait like a patient servant, called if needed, ignored if not. Maxim Litvinov, the Russian foreign minister, had for years sought alliances with the west, feeling that Germany was the savage beast in their midst, a beast that only an alliance of its powerful neighbors could keep tame.

But things are not necessarily what they would appear to be, and this would be the card that Hitler and Stalin would play.

The summer of 1939 ground on, filled with the tensions of a world that knew that soon it would be engulfed in war. To Poland war was a natural condition, so she took it calmly. Further it was a little like the weather—it had to be accepted but met with elegance and style.

Nonetheless, the peace efforts still came. The knowledge of impending war did not deter those last plays to salvage peace. Mussolini proposed another conference on the order of the 1938 meeting in Munich. Others, like Stalin and Hitler, were not interested, for they saw the profit to be gained from a properly managed war and looked upon it as a source of wealth and power.

Still others, like the French, had so much discord and had seen their land so ravaged in World War I, that they could neither unite to rescue peace nor, once the war had begun, fight it with the spirit needed to win. All they wanted was for war to go away, or at least to be over as quickly as possible. To the British the idea of war was so remote as to be almost unreal. Peace was the chance to continue business as usual, to hold the reins of empire, to rule and trade.

For at the time, what no one would see was the fact that in facing a man determined to make war, the only deterrent is to force him to accept peace by threatening to attack him first. This did not seem possible to France and Britain—the two nations that could carry it off. History would only prove that Hitler had been right. The French lacked the will, and the English on their own did not have the power. There was one other thing that might have stopped the Führer and that would have been for Russia to join Britain and France against him.

*At the end of August 1939, the German battleship* Schleswig-Holstein *arrived in Danzig harbor, where it was welcomed by the city's German population.*

Then came the bombshell of August 23, a few days before the planned invasion. The world was set agog by the news broadcast that morning: Russia and Germany had become friends and partners in trade. Two bitter enemies sworn to each others' destruction were now friends. What really would have set the world on its ear was the secret part of that accord, that Russia and Germany were now military allies and that to seal their treaty they had agreed on a fair division of Poland's spoils, roughly half and half. The Germans were to invade, and when they reached the state line, they would stop and wait for the Russians to come claim their half. This was the Soviet-German Nonaggresion Pact, better known as the Ribbentrop-Molotov Accord in honor of its authors.

Thus the laughable, the unthinkable had occurred. It left a jubilant Berlin and a dazed Europe in its wake. Hitler had gotten what he wanted. He had secured his rear. There would be no second front to worry about. The price had been high. He knew the Wehrmacht would do most of the fighting and that precious oil and other raw materials in the Baltic countries and Poland, materials essential to German war survival, had been given away to be bought later at exorbitant Russian prices. Stalin was a hard bargainer, Hitler now knew, and the bargains he would drive would be dear. But in the end it had been worth it. Besides, he had other plans for Russia, invasion plans he had only confided to a select few. All in good time. The important thing now was that the Russian threat had been neutralized.

Hitler's eagerness to move was almost unbridled now. He could not wait to show the French and the English what his Wehrmacht could do. For one thing he was convinced that the mere sight would set their hearts atrembling. If they would only understand that his real objective was in the east, that all he was doing was fulfilling Germany's destiny to expand and rule, no more. But they had to be shown. The terrible, dramatic scene he had masterminded would now be played.

CHAPTER VI

# BLITZKRIEG
# AND
# BETRAYAL

**O**n the night of August 31, 1939, the Mozart symphony being broadcast from the station at Gleiwitz near the Polish border was suddenly interrupted by a voice shouting patriotic slogans in Polish. Then came the sound of a scuffle, to be followed by shots. After that, silence.

To any gullible German listener this clearly meant that the anticipated Polish assault the German press had been predicting had finally taken place, and that the Gleiwitz station had been subdued by Polish forces. The hoax, if crude, would prove to be effective; it would be months before the truth was known. The "Polish forces" that had entered the station had, in fact, been SS men in Polish uniforms. These men fled when German units responded, but in the ensuing skirmish, they suffered losses. The "losses," it turned out, were condemned criminals who had been dressed to fit the part, shot, and had their bodies dumped in and around the station to dress the stage. Then the press was invited. Goebbels, in fact, had dreamed up this macabre ploy to show Western newsmen the extremes to which Polish arrogance would go and the consequential necessity of German countermeasures. To the assembled reporters—including one from the respected *New York Times*—the bodies were most convincingly dead; the incident, seemingly quite real. But why the Poles would stage such an attack when all the world knew that invasion was a thought in Hitler's not in Beck's mind was a mystery the Reich was not willing to explain. With the "rescue" of the Gleiwitz radio station, *Fall Weiss*—Case White, the invasion of Poland—was set in motion, exactly on the schedule the Führer himself had established. In the days that followed, over one million men, two thousand airplanes, and nearly three thousand tanks were hurled into what was to become a new kind of war.

The first shots were fired at 4:17 A.M. on the morning of September 1. A Nazi storming party, jumping the gun, attacked the main Danzig post office, manned by Poles. The fifty-one mailmen, however, were armed and put up a long and fierce resistance that would last most of the day.

Punctually at 4:45, the appointed hour for the attack, the *Schleswig-Holstein,* an old German battleship ostensibly in Danzig harbor on a goodwill visit, opened fire on the Westerplatte, a small fortified peninsula where a detachment of Polish marines was stationed. There were no other Polish troops in the city, only customs inspectors, border guards, and the like, for that had been one of the conditions the League of Nations had imposed: no military formations except the token force of eighty-eight Poles on the Westerplatte.

Strangely enough, though, artillery manned by German gunners began to appear, while what had appeared to be sporting clubs sprouted armed and uniformed men behaving suspiciously like Wehrmacht soldiers.

The *Schleswig-Holstein* kept pounding the Westerplatte fortifications. The batteries in Danzig joined in. For seven days the Poles, armed only with rifles, machine guns, and small cannon, held out; their fortification's ten-foot thick walls of reinforced concrete refused to cave in.

Finally, the Stuka dive-bombers were called in. In short order, their five hundred and fifty-pound bombs tore through the concrete. The Westerplatte surrendered. When the Polish commandant marched out, the German commander, in a tribute to the defender's heroism, allowed him to keep his sword. At least in the beginning of the war, there would still be a soldier's code.

Meanwhile, at the frontiers on that first day of September at 4:45 A.M., German units machine gunned Polish outposts and control stations and poured over the border. The tanks of the Panzer Divisions, spearheaded by motorcycles and armored cars, streamed forward. After them came the special motorized infantry, then foot soldiers ferried in every conceivable motor vehicle. After them came some cavalry; horse-drawn artillery followed, and finally the foot-slogging infantry.

These troops invaded in five columns spread over a fifteen-hundred-mile front. They came from Prussia, from Germany, from Austria, and from what once had been Czechoslovakia. They came from the north, the west, and the south. From Austrian, Czech, and German fields, the Stukas struck, their special sirens screaming death as they dived, magnifying the terror and the havoc their bombs would cause. Their first objective had been the Polish air force, much of which was caught still sitting on the ground. True, their fields near the frontier had been on a war footing, but deeper inland the air crews were having personnel and supply problems; they were not quite ready for what was to come.

Thanks to the French and the British, Polish mobilization was far from complete. "It will be seen by Hitler as a provocation," they had said. "Hold off." With great reluctance the Poles had agreed, not knowing that the German's own mobilization had been completed two weeks prior to the attack.

Now, Polish roads and railways were clogged with reservists reporting to their units, with matériel being distributed to various formations—the whole transportation network overstressed and overloaded. The result was that units went into combat undermanned, while the terrible Stukas—the job of bombing Polish airfields done—dropped their lethal loads on helpless men crammed in boxcars and horse-drawn wagons. Once the Stukas had gone and the Poles thought they

*Following the panzer divisions, columns of German horse-drawn artillery passed through the ravaged Polish countryside.*

had a respite, the Heinkel 123's, the "ein zwei dreis" came, flying so low the pilots' faces could be seen quite clearly as they throttled down their engines to gain maximum strafing time over their panicked targets.

The Luftwaffe seemed to be everywhere. In fact it was not so. A systematic plan had been established, and with great discipline it was being carried out. First, the plan called for the destruction of airports and the Polish planes on the ground. Not that the planes would matter much. The best the Poles had were their P7-11's, gull-winged monoplanes that in the early thirties would have put up a good fight. In 1939 they were outgunned, outrun, and outmaneuvered by most of what the Luftwaffe could provide. It had been a good plane, but not anymore. In any case there were to be too few of them. The scant survivors that escaped the ground attacks headed for Warsaw to defend the city and from there once more try their luck against hopeless odds.

The next Luftwaffe target had been command positions, crossroads, communication and transport hubs. And since Poland was industrially backward and poor, there were not many hubs. These targets went quite fast.

Then came the bombing and strafing of the Polish armies. After the first attack the Poles had to regroup in order to move, and in moving, they once more clogged the roads, making tempting targets for the Stukas. The cavalry brigades were particularly hard hit. The dust the horses raised was a beacon to the German pilots, who then homed in on their targets, their bullets and bombs tearing into man and horse alike as they desperately tried to race for cover. More than anything, the Polish horsemen prayed for trees and forests—a place to stop and rest, to regain their lost bearings. These were seldom to be found.

Neither the Polish people nor the nature of their terrain could withstand this kind of attack. In past wars there had always been a battle front, and behind that, staging and command areas. At the front the whole savagery of combat would run full tilt, while in the rear areas things would be quieter.

There the bustle of supply, of medical care, of troop deployment would show the more orderly, prosaic side of war. In this new kind of war, however, within hours there would be no front, no rear. On meeting the Polish lines, the Wehrmacht's Panzer columns did not bother to stop and fight. They punched their holes and poured through—running as fast as they could. Like long, lethal armored snakes, they were impervious to most of what the Poles could bring to bear. Relentlessly they drove on, bypassing strong points, heading for the Polish rear, where they created havoc and confusion. Polish divisions, even armies, were beheaded, their command posts destroyed. The leaderless units, left uncoordinated and without direction, were easy prey to second waves of Wehrmacht formations, which were at hand, ready for this task.

The surviving Poles were left totally disoriented, disorganized, and demoralized. They were like men in a weightless nightmare, never able to gain a foothold, never able to assume the initiative, never able to recover long enough to fight back effectively.

The Polish army was the classic example of a poor nation's force. Composed primarily of infantry and cavalry, it had grossly neglected the development of communications as well as of fire power. Lacking radio systems, it relied on couriers and the civilian telephone and telegraph network. The former were slow and ineffectual except at very short distances, and the latter were traditionally the first elements to break down in combat conditions.

Polish firepower, that is, the ability of any unit to hurl ordnance at an enemy, was about half that of an equivalent German formation. Their antitank guns were few and far between, while the nearly total absence of antiaircraft batteries was sorely felt in that September.

Unlike any other Western nation, Poland had maintained an unusually large cavalry, feeling that the nature of Polish soil, its weather, and the primitive state of most of its roads would give the mounted soldier an edge over his motorized

*Tanks of a Wehrmacht panzer division roll through
Poland during the invasion that
gave the world its first experience with blitzkrieg.*

counterpart. Besides, Polish cavalry had distinguished itself always, the last time in the Russo-Polish War of 1920. Cavalry had then been a major factor for both sides, Semyon Budenny's cossacks ravaging Poland, only to be repelled by Polish *uhlans*. The idea of an army without the clatter of hoofs and sabers, without lances and pennons was unthinkable.

Poland in 1939 had about eight hundred tanks versus the Wehrmacht's nearly three thousand. These were scattered, used basically as motorized artillery for infantry divisions. They were mostly early French units which, while not as mobile as the Panzers, were in some cases better armored or gunned.

The Poles, however, were confident that a disciplined and experienced soldier who was well motivated could match anything the Reich could field. While this concept might have been true in an earlier time, the Wehrmacht proved that tanks, dive bombers, excellent communications, and a brilliant plan of action would make that soldier's heroic stand a futile task.

The Poles had felt secure, even arrogant as they waited. After all, had they not within a single generation fought not only most of their smaller neighbors, but mighty Russia as well? And had they not defeated them all, including the Soviet army? They knew full well the price of war in pain, bloodshed, and mourning. But they also knew that steadfastness, heroism, and initiative could snatch victory from the jaws of defeat. And Poland, they felt, had an ample supply of these fine qualities.

So it was that on September 1 they had almost eagerly awaited the Wehrmacht's attack. Their plan had been simple. Polish forces would be massed at the borders and then would slowly retreat, keeping casualties as low as possible, since the object was to gain time: time first for her allies, France and Britain, to declare war—an act they had agreed would take place on the third invasion day. Then still more time for French forces to attack Germany's vulnerable western flank, forcing the Germans to fight the dreaded two-front war. The Poles expected heavy losses both in manpower and in territory, but they felt that with this plan they could not only contain a German attack but that their heroic behavior would be rewarded by the Allies with large chunks of a defeated Germany.

But the Polish cup was not to be so easily drained. With a recently renewed nonagression treaty, the thought that Russia would attack at this juncture was not considered likely by Warsaw.

Although their relations with the Russians had been extremely correct, the Poles did not wish to see a single Soviet soldier on their soil, even if it was to help. Their entire diplomatic effort, therefore, had been aimed at maintaining Russian neutrality.

All these plans and conclusions, of course, would prove to be quite incorrect, for not only had Hitler made sure of the Soviets' cooperation, but the Wehrmacht was waging a new kind of war.

In the 1930s few generals outside Germany had thought of war in any other than the trench warfare terms of World War I. They had seen the carnage of that war and the pitifully few yards any offensive had yielded before everyone dug in again. Defense had reigned supreme in 1918, and they saw no real reason to think differently now. The best example of this was the Maginot Line, a series of impregnable French fortifications facing the German border.

Analyzing the results of 1918, the German General Staff concluded that even it if could quickly mobilize all its resources, Germany could not win a prolonged war. It lacked the essential elements in foodstuffs and raw materials to do so. Therefore, they reasoned, the effort must be made to make any war in which it engaged one where the elements of surprise, mobility, and concentration of firepower would have the most telling effect. The German armies must march quickly, bypass strong points, with lightning strikes destroy the enemy's nerve centers, and only then consolidate their gains.

Two developments of World War I would reinforce their thinking. These were the airplane and the tank.

The Allies had been conscious, too, of the potential impact of these weapons and had ordered the surrender or total destruction of all the Reich's aircraft and armor. But the future they had seen was not the same future the Germans saw.

The Allies envisioned huge fleets of bombers destroying entire cities. As an example of this terror, they cited Guernica, a Spanish town that had been destroyed by bombs in 1938, bombing that made so deep an impression that Pablo Picasso dedicated one of his most famous paintings to it. What the Allied strategists had failed to note was that the anticipated effect of this terror bombing had *not* taken place, that instead of losing their backbone, the survivors were if anything strengthened in their determination to continue fighting.

To the Germans, who had mounted the raid on Guernica, the results had borne out their own thinking. A better use of airpower was as a ground support weapon. Use it for reconnaissance and strafing, but most of all, use it as extremely accurate long-range artillery. From this reasoning the Stuka dive-bomber was born. Later on, when the Luftwaffe strayed from these concepts, its results would be quite poor; when it adhered to them, it would meet with great success.

But the Germans did not stop there in their new vision of war. If the havoc that planes created was to be exploited, special ground forces would be needed to finish the job. These had to be self-protected, extremely mobile columns with vast firepower. In other words, armored Panzer divisions. To be effective, though, they would have to be used in concentrated formations and deployed in hitherto unpracticed ways.

In France Captain Charles de Gaulle, who would later become president of his country, was writing and lecturing to this effect in the war college. In England a handful of men had seen the same light. Yet all were ignored by their commanders. In high British and French military circles the concept of the tank was as self-propelled artillery for marching infantry and as a mobile fort around which the foot soldiers could rally.

Ironically, it would take Heinz Guderian—a German infantry officer born in what in 1939 was Poland, and reared in Alsace-Lorraine, which after 1918 had become a part of France—to fully conceive of this kind of war. He fully grasped the concepts of tank warfare and put them together as a new military thought, a thought that would come to be called "Blitzkrieg," or literally, lightning war.

To function effectively the approach would require—besides mechanized mobility and vast firepower—superb coordination, excellent communication systems, and large supplies. Most of all, though, it would demand decisiveness, boldness, and daring—characteristics that were conspicuous in their absence from British and French military thinking.

Battered but not vanquished, the Poles retreated, abandoning most of Poland west of Warsaw If they only could hold out, they thought, the French and British would begin to pound Germany on her western front and then Poland could assume the offensive.

And so September 3 arrived and with it the welcome Allied declaration of war. In the rubbled Warsaw streets people gathered and marched off to the British and French embassies. There they proudly sang "God Save the King" and the "Marsellaise" with tears in their eyes, in emotion-choked, Polish-accented voices.

Now the Germans would see, with their Stukas and their panzers, they reassured each other, now they would see. And with renewed hope they resumed the fighting. They were confident that even though they were too far away to be seen or heard, squadrons of British Blenheim bombers would be flying over Essen, making the Krupp works, Europe's largest armorer, erupt in smoke and fire, much as Warsaw was now doing. They could envision the ships and docks at Bremen and Hamburg going up in flames and Hitler's legions turning back. Turning back to meet the French Somuas and Char C's, huge tanks bigger, yet as fast as anything the Wehrmacht had.

But the Allied help would never come. No rescue trains, no second front, no bombed German cities to share the price of war. Poland was too far, the Allies too fearful, their leadership blind to the realities that Blitzkrieg had unleashed. The British bombers limited their flights to dropping leaflets to demoralize the Germans and to one unfortunate attack on German warships, where their deadly cargo bounced off the ships' armored decks while three Blenheim bombers were shot down. On the ground the French were still mobilizing, they said, but orders had gone out to keep the men at the frontier from shooting at any German in anger. Most historians (and German generals) are agreed that at this juncture an Allied attack on Germany's western fortifications along the Siegfried Line would have succeeded, for the pillboxes, forts, and tank traps not only were incomplete but also were grossly undermanned. Even little Renault R7 tanks could have gotten through, for there were no panzers to oppose them, and much of the artillery for the forts was either in Poland or still at the Krupp or Skoda factories.

So while on the eastern front the Poles were methodically being crushed, on the west Hitler's biggest weapons were loudspeakers that blared in French, "If you don't shoot we won't shoot either; why pay with French blood for Polish outrages; remember the British motto, 'We shall fight to the last Frenchman.' " Of the last, the Frenchmen were keenly aware, for in World War I, most of the fighting had taken place on French soil. Indeed, in this war it would be December before the first British soldier would die in combat. Meanwhile, in full sight, or sometimes modestly behind huge mats, German troops continued to work uninterruptedly on the Siegfried Line, or West Wall, as it would sometimes be called.

By the fifth day of the invasion, Hitler, who was inspecting the front, would agree with General Franz Halder of the

OKW, the Wehrmacht's High Command, who wrote in his diary, "As of today, the enemy is practically beaten." Recognizing this, the OKW would begin the redeployment process to shift the troops to the West Wall.

The Poles, however, did not see things this clearly. Any time now the rains would come, and with them the air attacks would cease; the panzers would bog down in Polish mud, the French attack would come; and once again it would be Poland's day.

But it was not to be. The skies stayed clear and bright, the footing firm and flat. The mighty rivers were still fordable, so Stukas and panzers could, unhampered, continue their field exercise. Days passed and the noose grew ever tighter. By September 16 only Warsaw was holding out. Here and there detachments still fought, but nothing that worried the Germans; indeed, they had already begun their pullout.

And then, on September 17, the surprise came. Across the eastern border Soviet troops came streaming, some shouting "Tovarich, Comrade, we've come to help you" before mowing down the astonished Polish soldiers. The Russians had at last come to claim their share.

The move, however, had taken extensive German urging. Stalin was a cautious man. He demurred, he played for time. He said he wanted to wait until Warsaw had fallen. Then, he felt, he could come in, ostensibly to protect the Ukrainian and Byelorussian minorities. For one thing, he had to consider that it might be a trap, that the Germans could lure him into Poland only to close in on his overextended lines. For another thing, the longer the Wehrmacht was engaged, the more Germans would be dead, which suited Stalin just fine.

For his part, Hitler was, indeed, not being polite when he invited Stalin to march in. More than anything he needed to show the Allies that this time there would not be an eastern threat, that Germany was not going to face a two-front war. He also wanted the democracies to see that there would be no use in wooing Russia. To that end he wanted Russian

*Weapons from the defeated Poles are
piled in a public square in Warsaw.*

hands to be soaked in Polish blood, thus committing the Reds to the Reich's camp.

In spite of Stalin's determination to wait, the battlefield successes were too much for him. The Germans were first approaching and then crossing the line agreed upon as the meeting ground for German and Russian forces. Polish resistance was collapsing with increasing speed. Soon all the country would be overwhelmed by the Wehrmacht. With such astonishing successes Hitler might renege on his agreement. So Stalin took the risk, and sent the Red army racing into Poland.

In Soviet history books the event came to be described as a rescue mission to the Poles, Russia extending a helping hand to a fellow Slav. Of the Russo-German treaty there is scarcely a mention, of the secret protocol that spelled out the Soviet-German military alliance, not a word. No word of Soviet-German deals. Only silence.

Warsaw held out until the end of September. Bombed daily, surrounded by massed panzers, the city would not give in until its supplies ran out, until its last P7-11 fighter had been shot down. In the countryside Polish lancers tried to engage Wehrmacht units, only to be repulsed by Stuka or panzer counterattacks.

For the Germans it had been a brief and brilliant war. The Russians, too, were pleased; much of Poland was now theirs. Blitzkrieg and betrayal had worked extremely well when marched together, hand in hand.

# AFTERMATH

**O**ctober came, and with it the long awaited rains and the end of the Polish campaign. For the Poles, though, defeat did not bring a respite. Sixty seven thousand Poles had fallen on the field, two hundred thousand were Russian prisoners, seven hundred thousand more were being packed off to work in Germany for the glory of the Reich and very short rations. One hundred thousand would manage to escape to fight another day. The Germans left behind fourteen thousand dead; the Russians lost only seven hundred men.

For those Poles who stayed or were left behind, the Führer had made very special plans. The first step was to exterminate the intelligentsia, a term most democratically applied. Not only did it include writers and professors, artists and clergymen, but it also covered nearly anyone who had had a higher education or who could be conceived of as a potential leader.

Next would come the solution to the Jewish problem, no small matter, since Poland had three million Jews. In the beginning, Jews were deported, isolated in walled-in ghettos and shot in mass executions. Later, in a frantic quest for effi-ciency, Hitler created those tragic monuments to inhumani-ty—the extermination camps. Zyclone B gas and mass crema-tions were the stock in trade for Auschwitz, Treblinka, Belsen, and others. Here two thirds of Poland's Jewry would perish, together with many of their non-Polish brethren.

The few Poles who were left were categorized as subhuman, to be used as tools or beasts of toil.

In order to administer these newly acquired possessions, the Germans annexed outright all of western Poland. This they would Germanize by settling into it Germanic people from the Baltic countries Hitler had given to Stalin. Since Estonia, Latvia, and Lithuania had substantial Germanic populations who were now in need of homes, the number of dead and exiled Jews and Poles had to at least equal that of the newcomers.

Central Poland was designated the "General Government" under German rule, and became the catchbasin for all conquered Europe. Here the undesirables would be confined until they could be transferred to the death camps.

Eastern Poland, by previous agreement, was Russia's, and the Soviets were not much kinder than the Germans. In the Katyn Forest near Smolensk in Russia, they shot and buried the remnants of the Polish officer corps that had fallen in their hands. Untold thousands of other Poles simply disappeared into Siberia.

Yet for a short while the Poles would be avenged in Finland, when seventy thousand Finns took on the massed might of the Red army. When the inevitable came, there were two hundred thousand frozen Russian corpses to show that the Soviets' path would not always be as easy as it had been in Poland, where the Wehrmacht's Blitzkrieg had paved the Russian's way.

In September 1939, the Allies had declared war on Germany. For months, the French and Germans waged the "Phony War," in which they assured each other that they meant no harm and avoided actual combat as much as possible. But in the spring Hitler would march. In two short months the Wehrmacht would liquidate by brilliant generalship a large, better armed foe. The Belgians, the Dutch, the French, the English, all would be defeated. Their remnants would be pushed against a rocky beach called Dunkirk and from there thrown across the English Channel.

The Reich and its unholy ally, Russia, appeared invincible. With his rear secured, and with the resources of nearly all of Western Europe in his hands, Hitler believed he could not only last out a long, prolonged war—long a German nightmare—but even win it.

With these victories his contempt for the democracies rose, and his feeling that the west was weak and spent seemed justified. The democracies, he thought, lacked the substance, the soil that breeds great men. Nowhere except in Russia's Stalin did he see a man to approach—let alone match—his own stature. As he surveyed the smoking ruins of what once had been a proud Polish nation, and as he prepared to launch the Wehrmacht's legions to finish off a dispirited Western Europe, he could see no one with the strength to oppose him.

He did not yet know that from those despised democracies a voice would soon rise, a Herculean voice from an overweight, cigar-smoking man with a twinkle in his eye. Hitler could not know this man would rally his people and a world behind him to oppose and in the end thwart the Führer's dream. Nor could Hitler imagine that Winston Churchill would achieve his aim without appealing to man's baser instincts, without catering to hatred, greed, or fear. Churchill would instead call forth from his nation and from the world, a response to man's highest aspirations; he would ask them to honor nobility of mind, strength of faith, and loftiness of spirit—things that to Hitler were but gossamer ghosts, utterly useless against screaming Stukas or death-dealing panzer divisions.

We know the outcome.

# FOR FURTHER READING

Barker, Elizabeth. *Austria 1918–1972.* Coral Gables, Florida: University of Miami Press, 1973.

Bennett, J.W. Wheeler. *Nemesis of Power.* New York: St. Martin's Press, 1967.

Bethell, Nicholas A. *The War Hitler Won.* New York: Holt Rinehart & Winston, 1972.

Brogan, D.W. *The French Nation 1914–1940.* New York: Harper & Brothers, 1957.

Cuff, James H. *The Face of the War.* New York: Julian Messner, 1942.

Deighton, Len. *Blitzkrieg.* New York: Alfred A. Knopf, 1980.

Deighton, Len. *Fighter.* New York: Alfred A. Knopf, 1978.

Dobroszycki and Kirshenblatt-Gimblett, Barbara. *Image Before My Eyes.* New York: Schocken Books, 1977.

Elson, Robert T. *Prelude To War.* Alexandria, Virginia: Time-Life Books, Inc., 1976.

Gilbert, Felix. *The End of the European Era 1890 to the Present.* New York: W.W. Norton & Company, 1979.

Guderian, Heinz. *Panzer Leader.* New York: Ballantine Books, 1957.

Halecki, O. *A History of Poland.* New York: Roy Publishers, 1966.

Herzstein, R.E. *The Nazis.* Alexandria, Virginia: Time-Life Books, Inc., 1980.

Hughes, H. Stuart. *Contemporary Europe*. Englewood Cliffs, New Jersey: Prentice-Hall, Inc., 1961.

Mason, Herbert Molloy Jr. *The Rise of the Luftwaffe 1918–1940*. New York: Dial Press, 1973.

Mowat, Charles Loch. *Britain Between the Wars 1918–1940*. Chicago: University of Chicago Press, 1961.

Newmann, Peter. *The Black March*. New York: William Sloane Associates, 1959.

Piekalkiewicz, Janusz. *The Cavalry of World War II*. Briarcliff Manor, New York: Stein & Day, 1980.

Rozek, Edward J. *Allied Wartime Diplomacy*. New York: John Wiley & Sons, 1958.

Shirer, William L. *Berlin Diary*. New York: Alfred A. Knopf, 1941.

Shirer, William L. *The Rise and Fall of the Third Reich*. New York: Simon and Schuster, 1960.

Snyder, Louis L. *The War—A Concise History, 1939–1945*. New York: Julian Messner, 1961.

Speer, Albert. *Inside the Third Reich*. New York: The Macmillan Company, 1970.

Stetson-Watson, Hugh. *Eastern Europe 1918–1941*. Hamden, Connecticut: Archon Books, Cambridge University Press, 1962.

Tolland, John. *Adolf Hitler*. New York: Doubleday, 1976.

Watt, Richard M. *Bitter Story: Poland and Its Fate 1918–1939*. New York: Simon & Schuster, 1979.

Wernick, Robert. *Blitzkrieg*. Alexandria, Virginia: Time-Life Books, Inc., 1977.

Young, Desmond. *Rommel, the Desert Fox*. New York: Harper & Row, 1951.

_____. *Poland: The Country and Its People*. Warsaw: Interpress Publishers,

# INDEX